I dedicate this little coloring book for children to God. In this world with so much technology, I hope that our children will disconnect a little from their cell phones and tablets and literally put their hands on colored pencils, brushes, and paint pots.
I thank my beloved wife, mother, and grandmother Angela for her encouragement and support. I love you!

Sergio Lourenço
2024

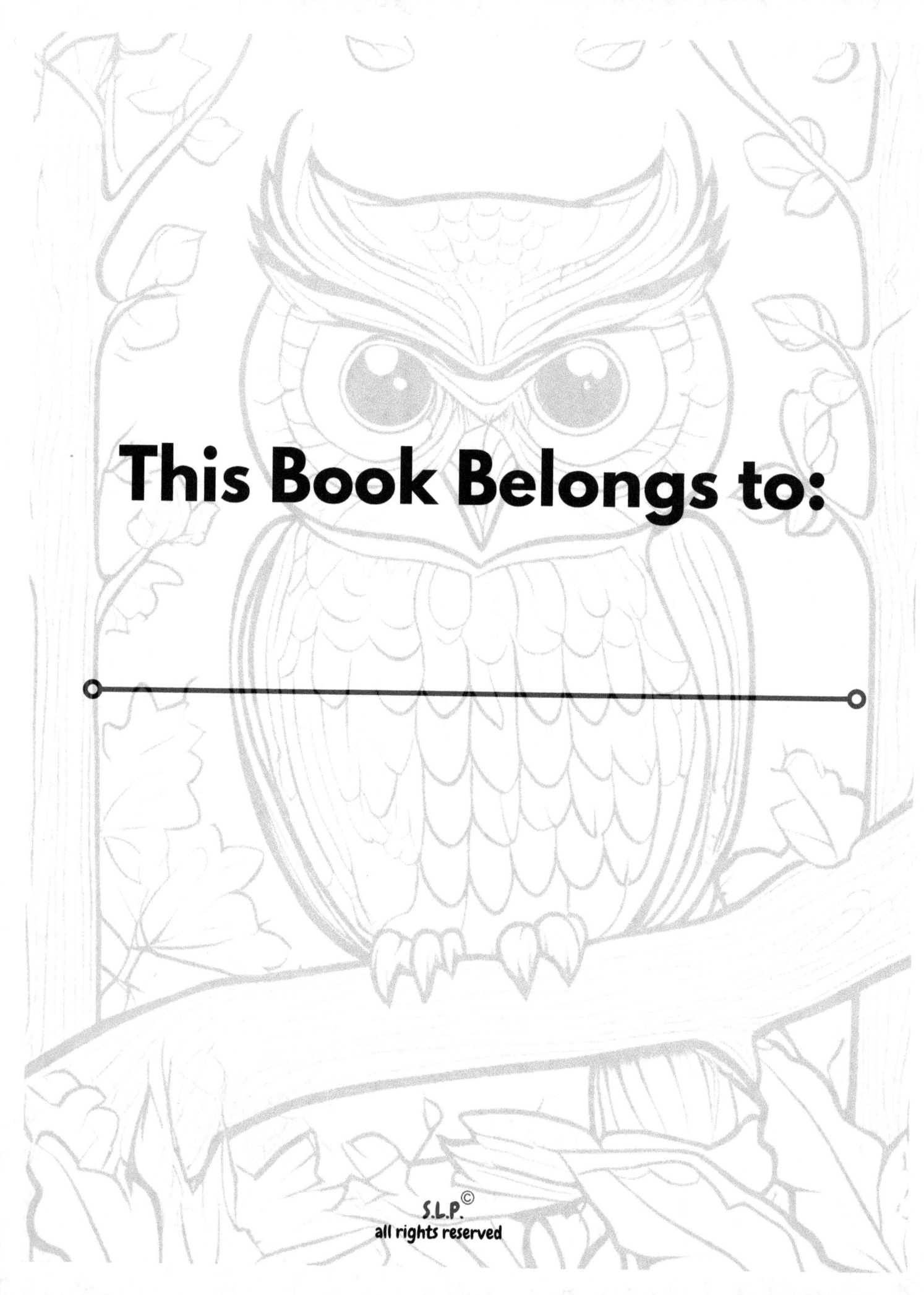

This Book Belongs to:

Test Color Page

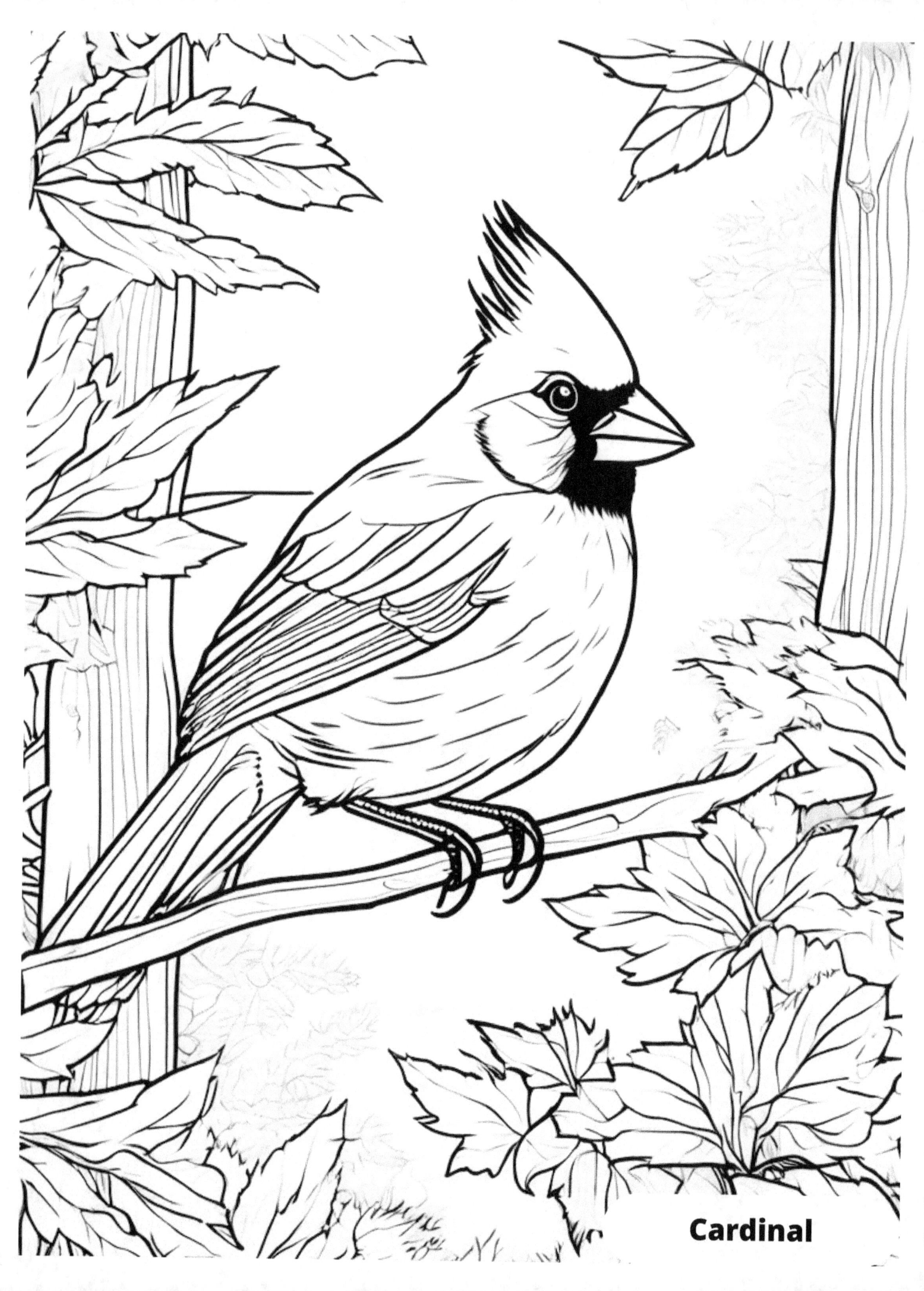

Cardinal

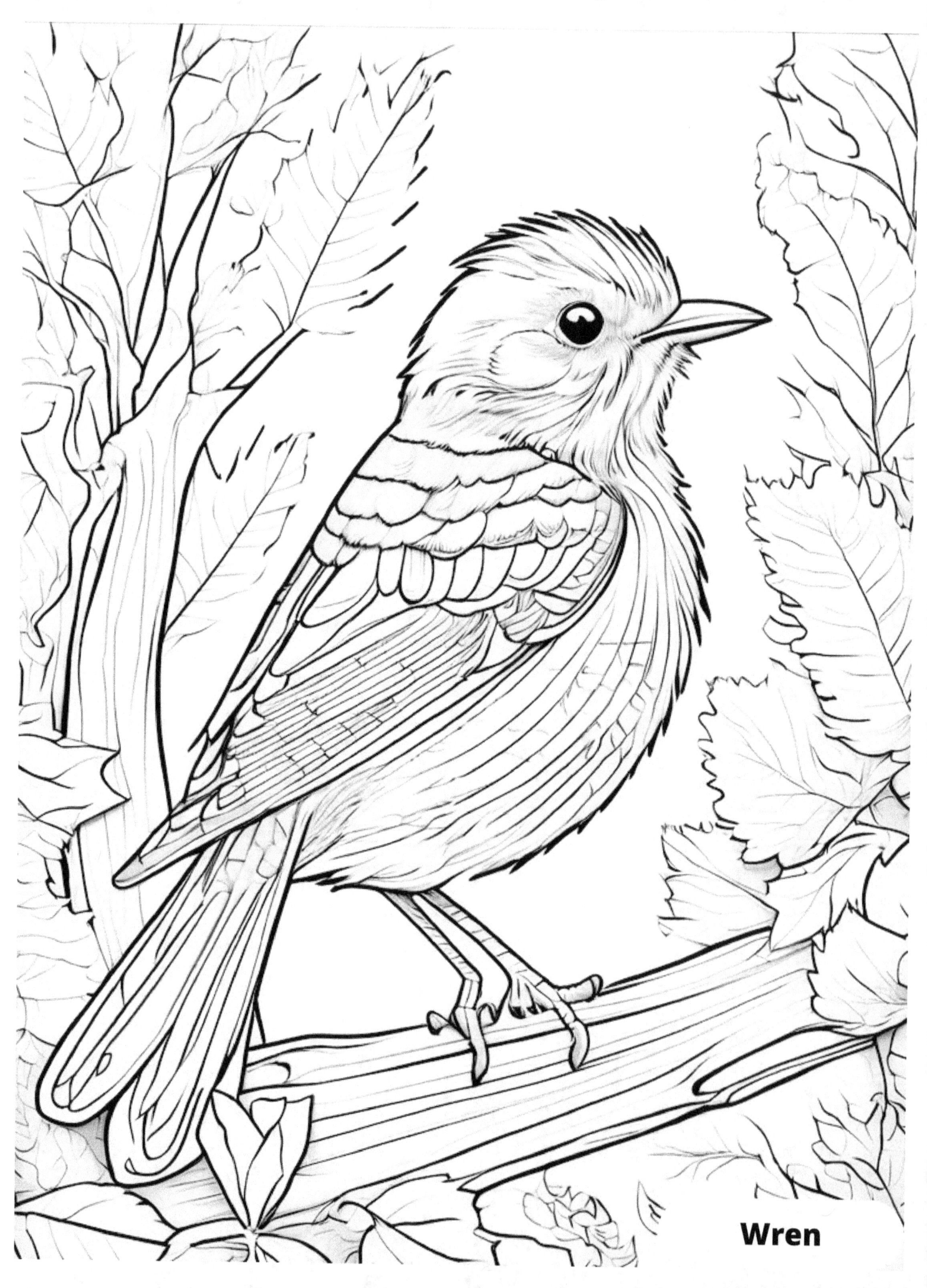

Wren

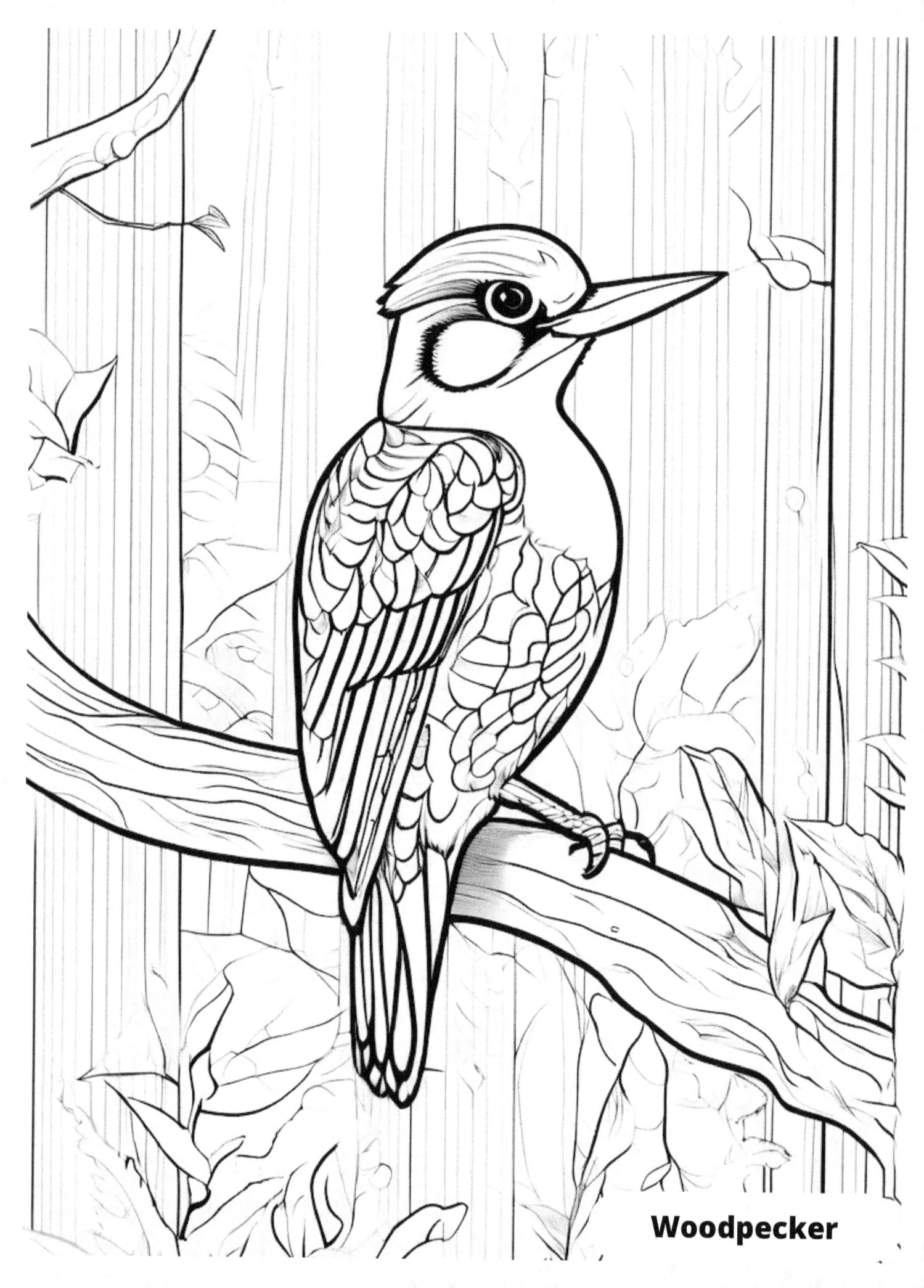

Woodpecker

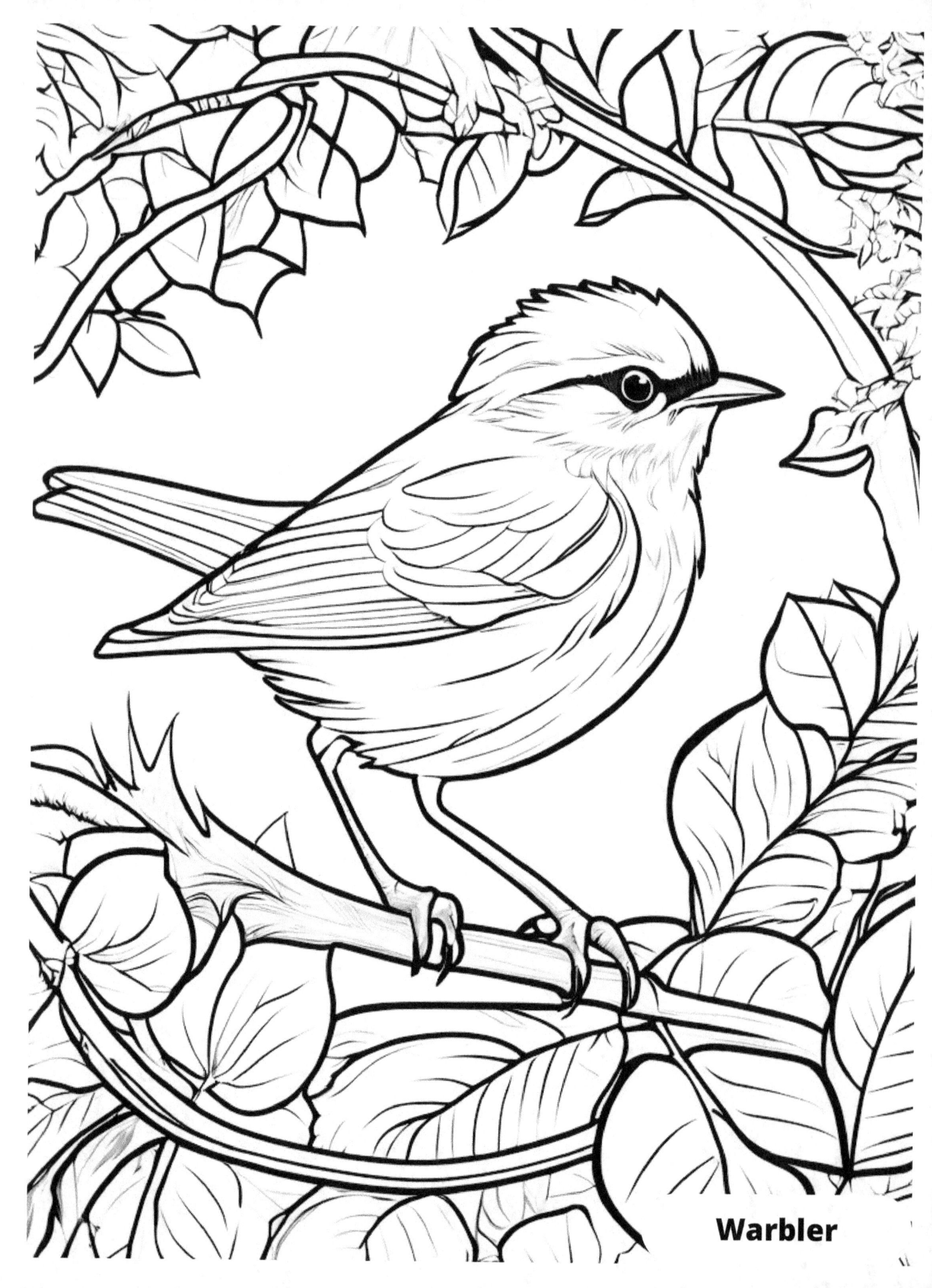

Warbler

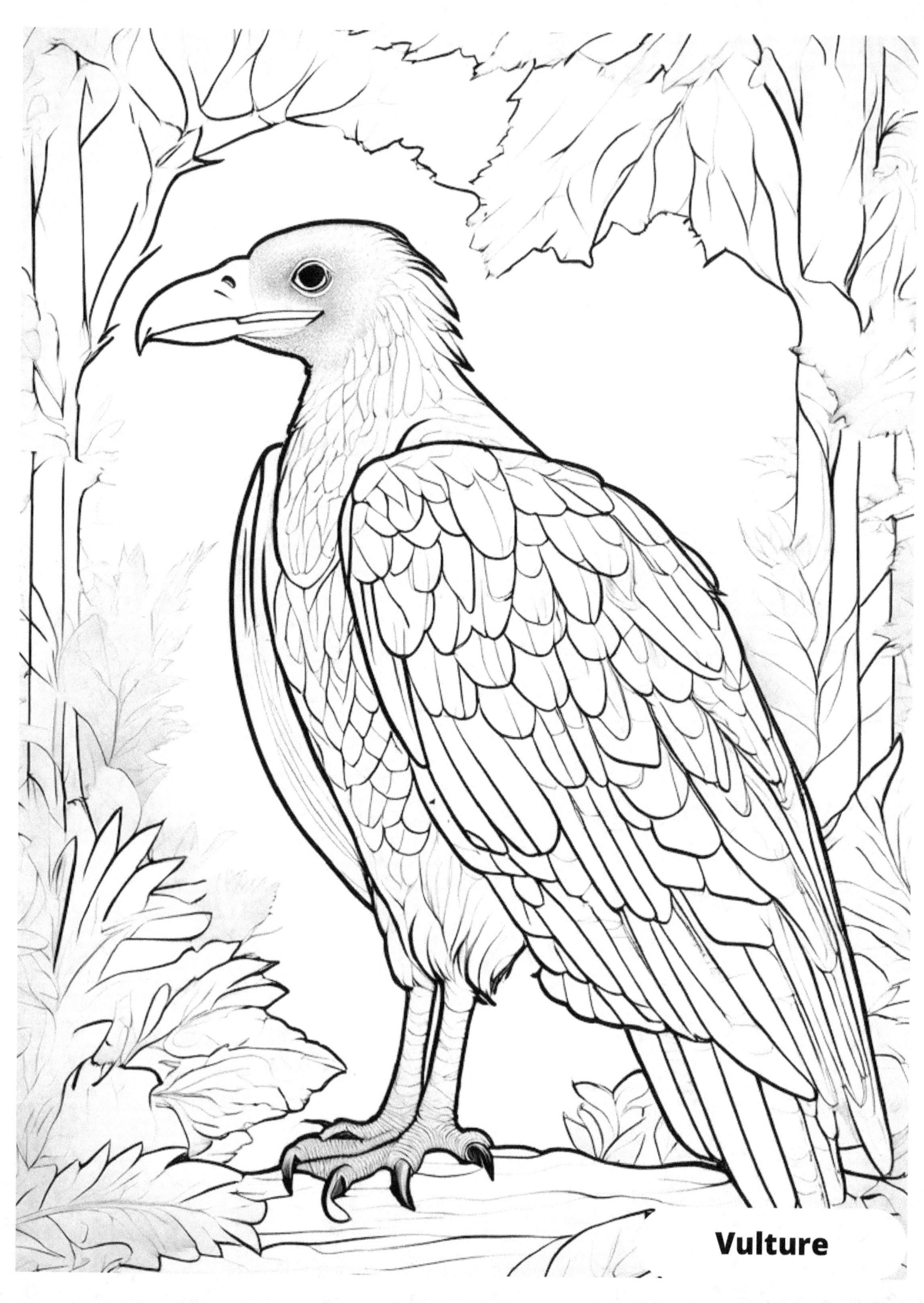

Vulture

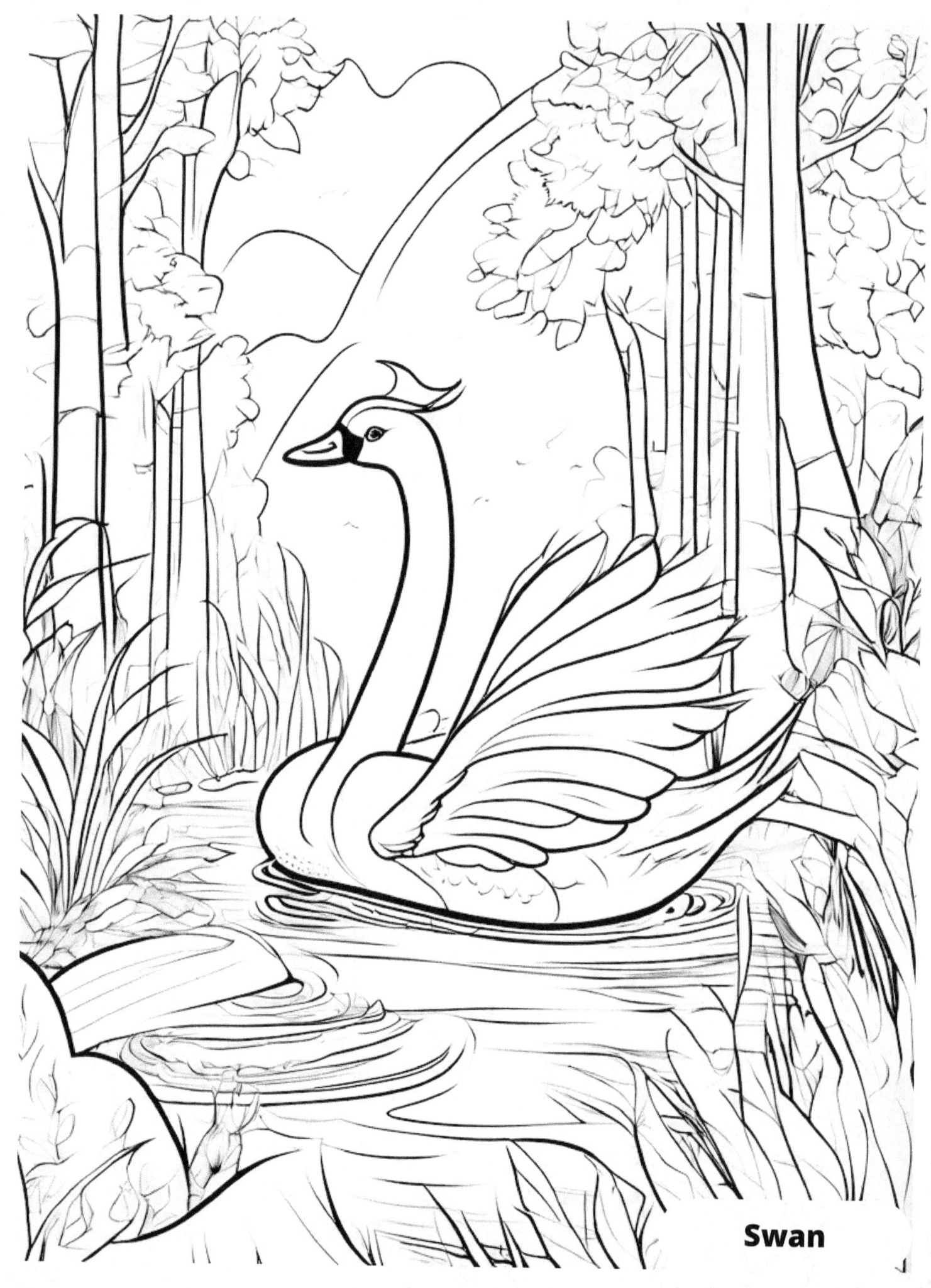

Swan

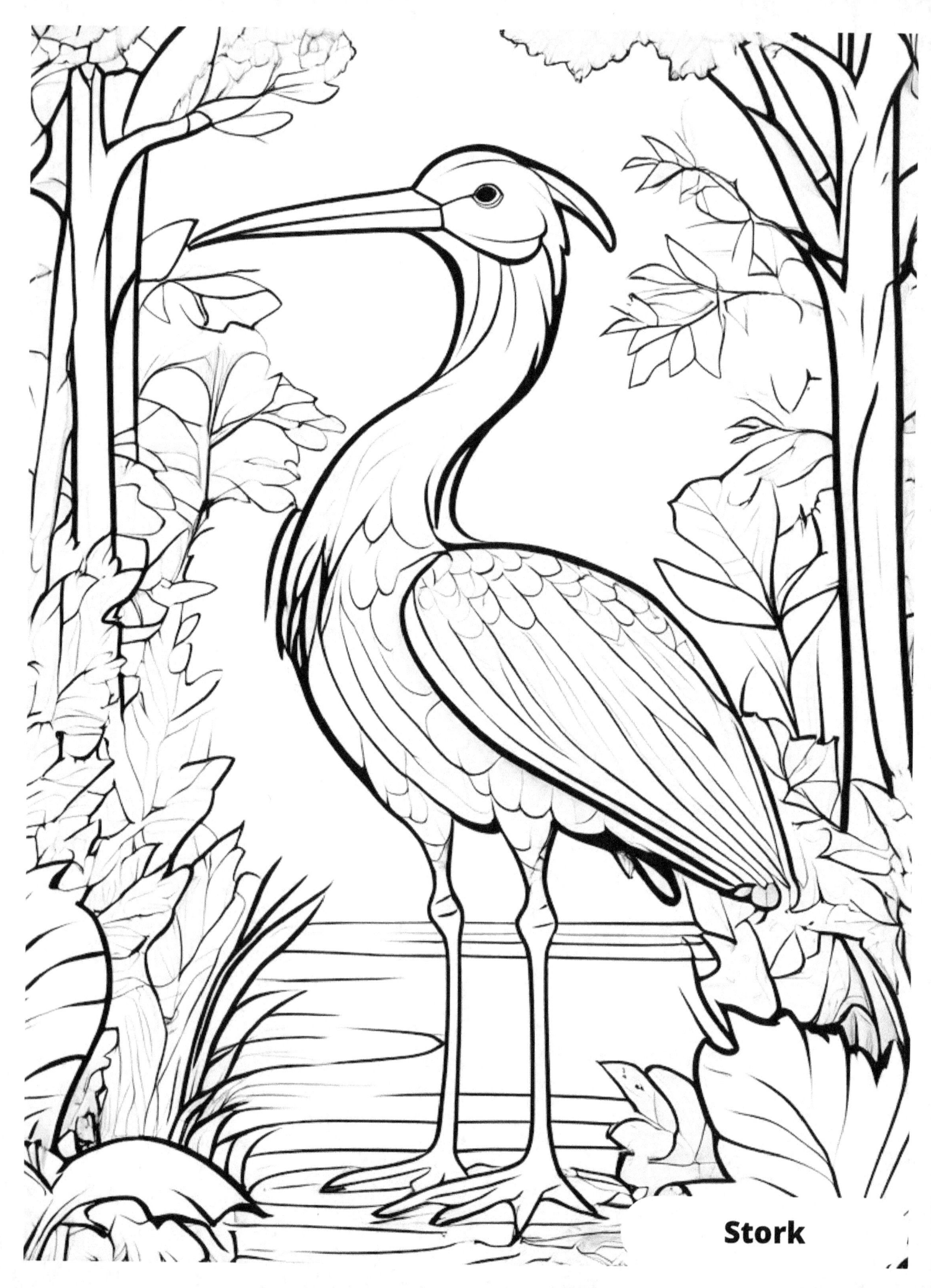

Stork

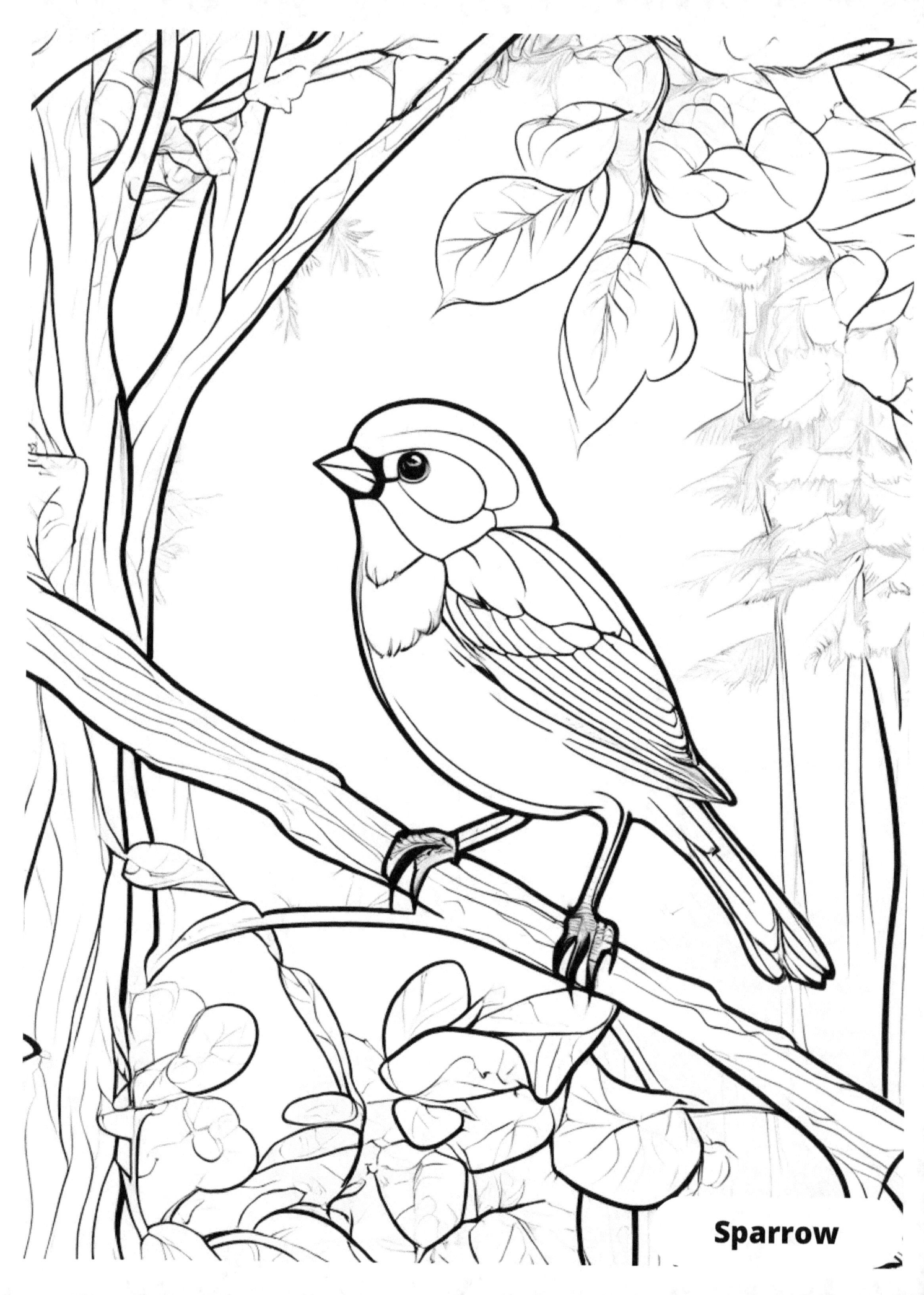

Sparrow

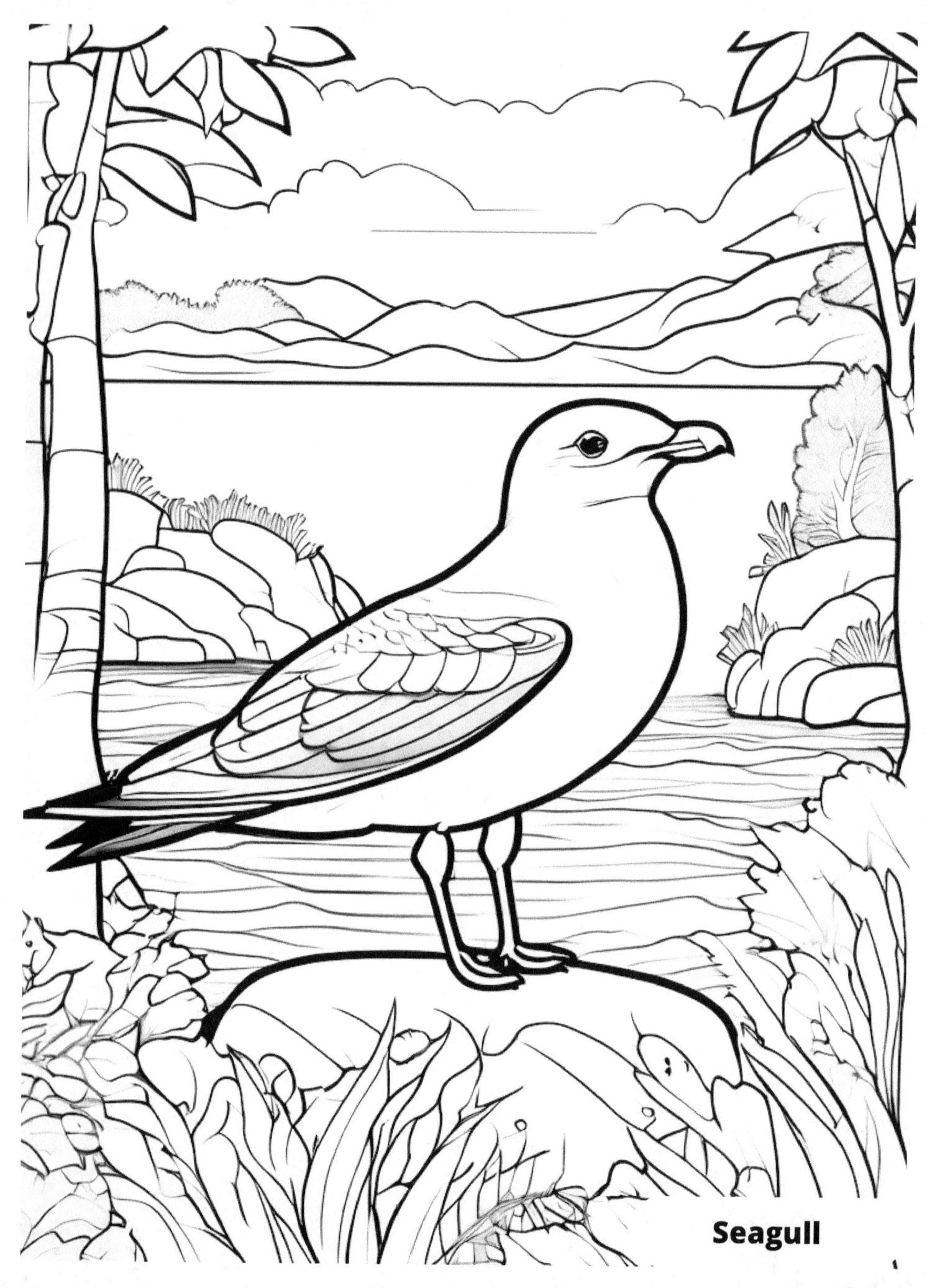

Seagull

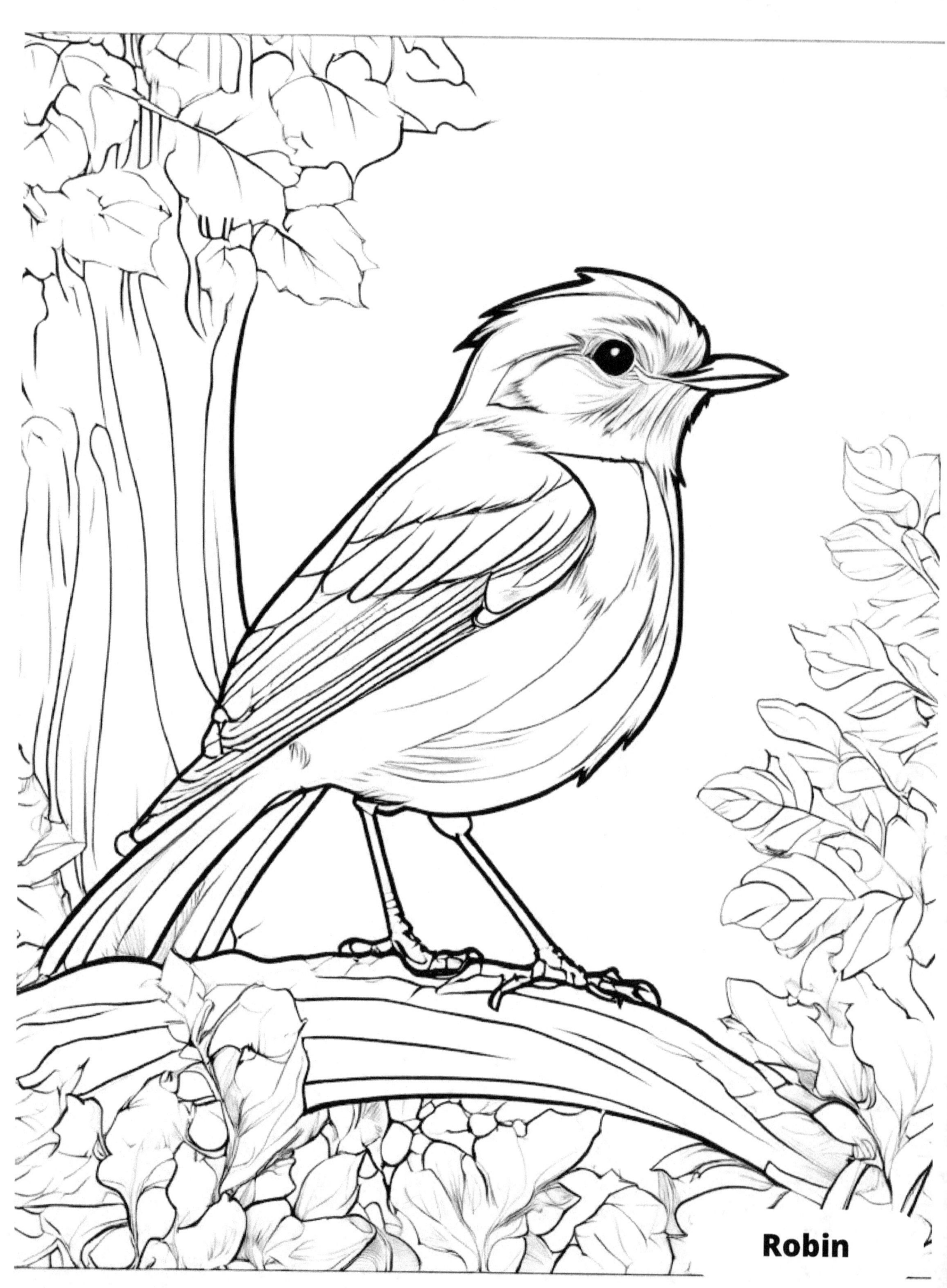

Robin

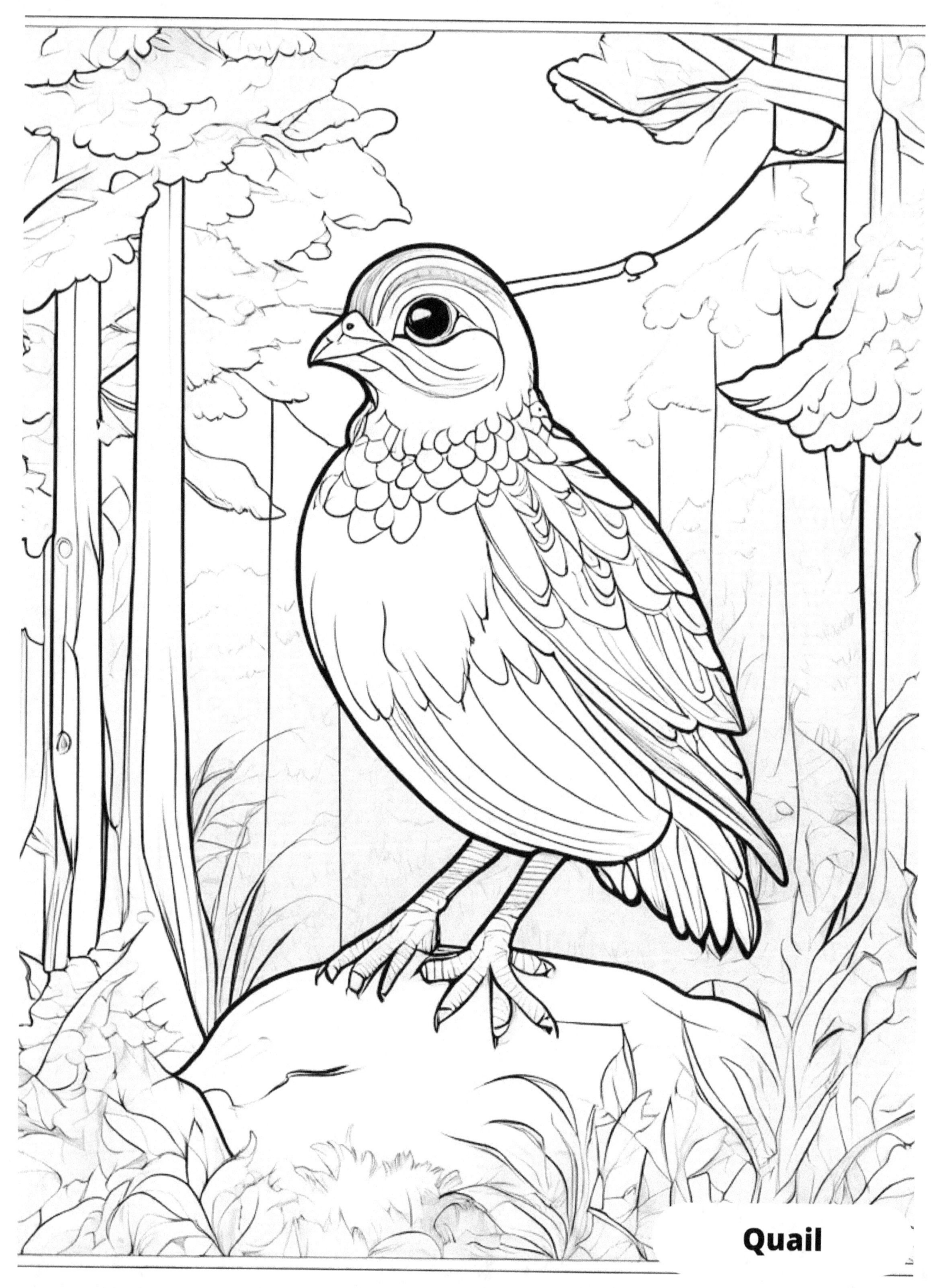

Quail

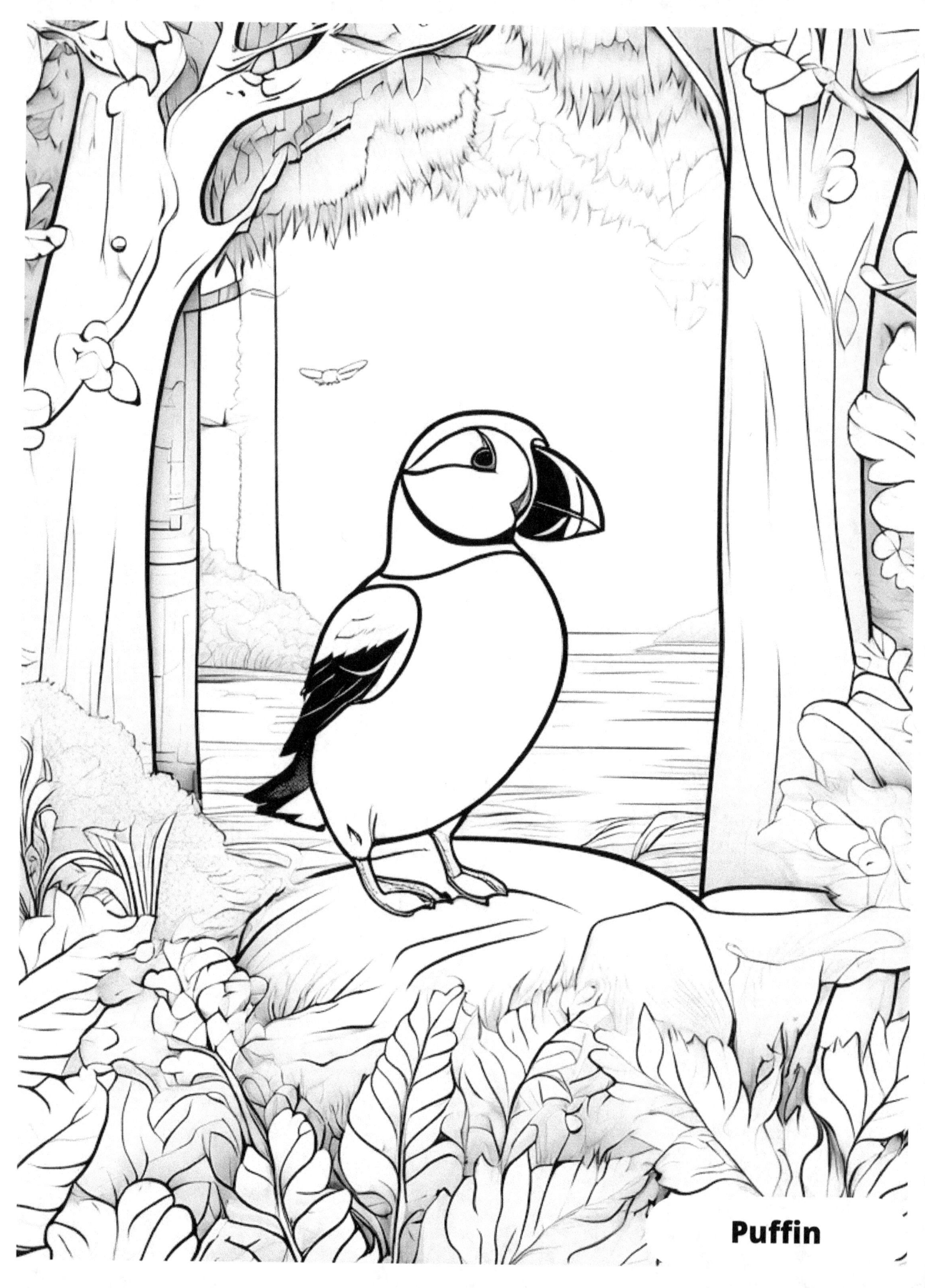

Puffin

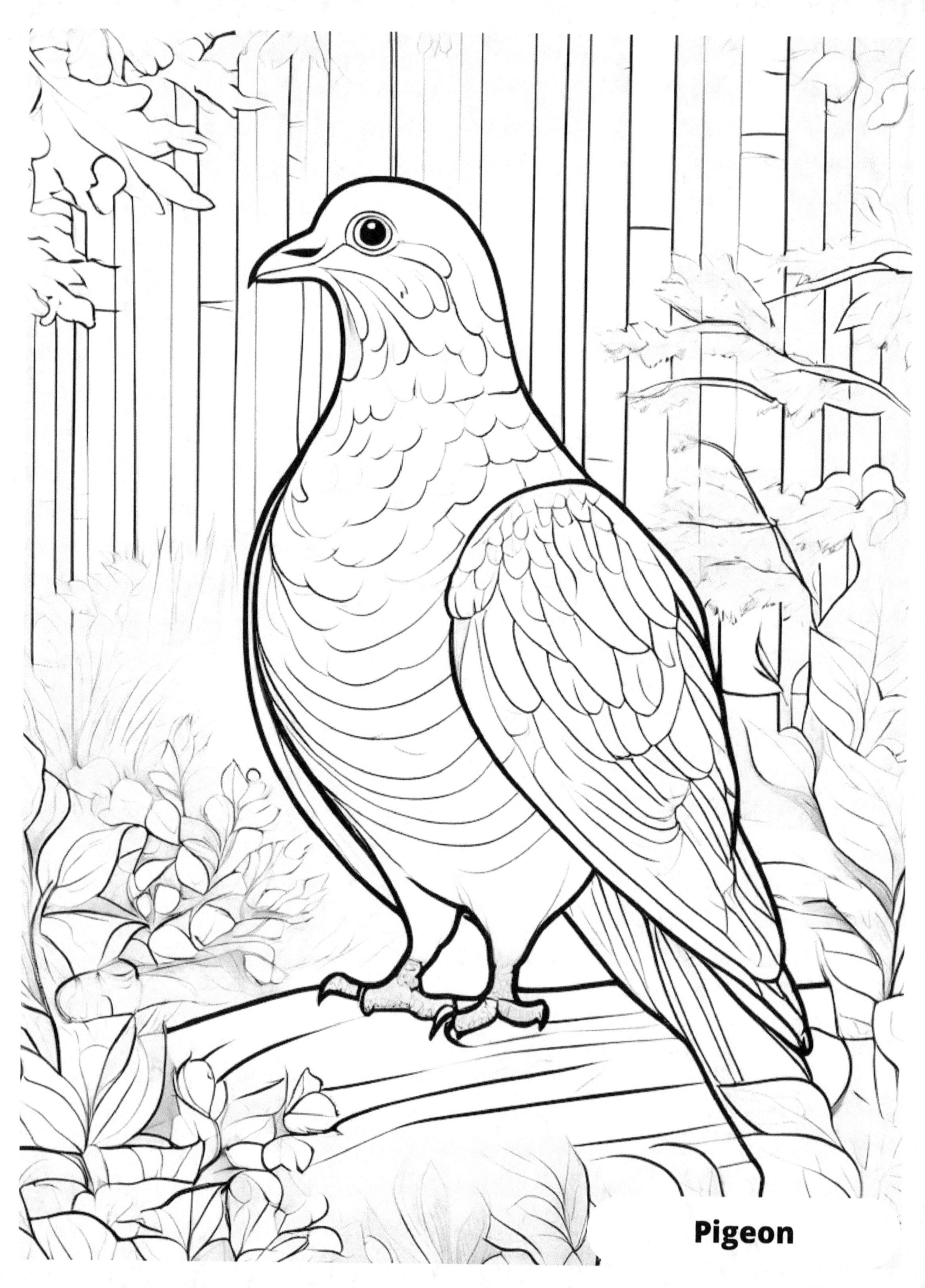

Pigeon

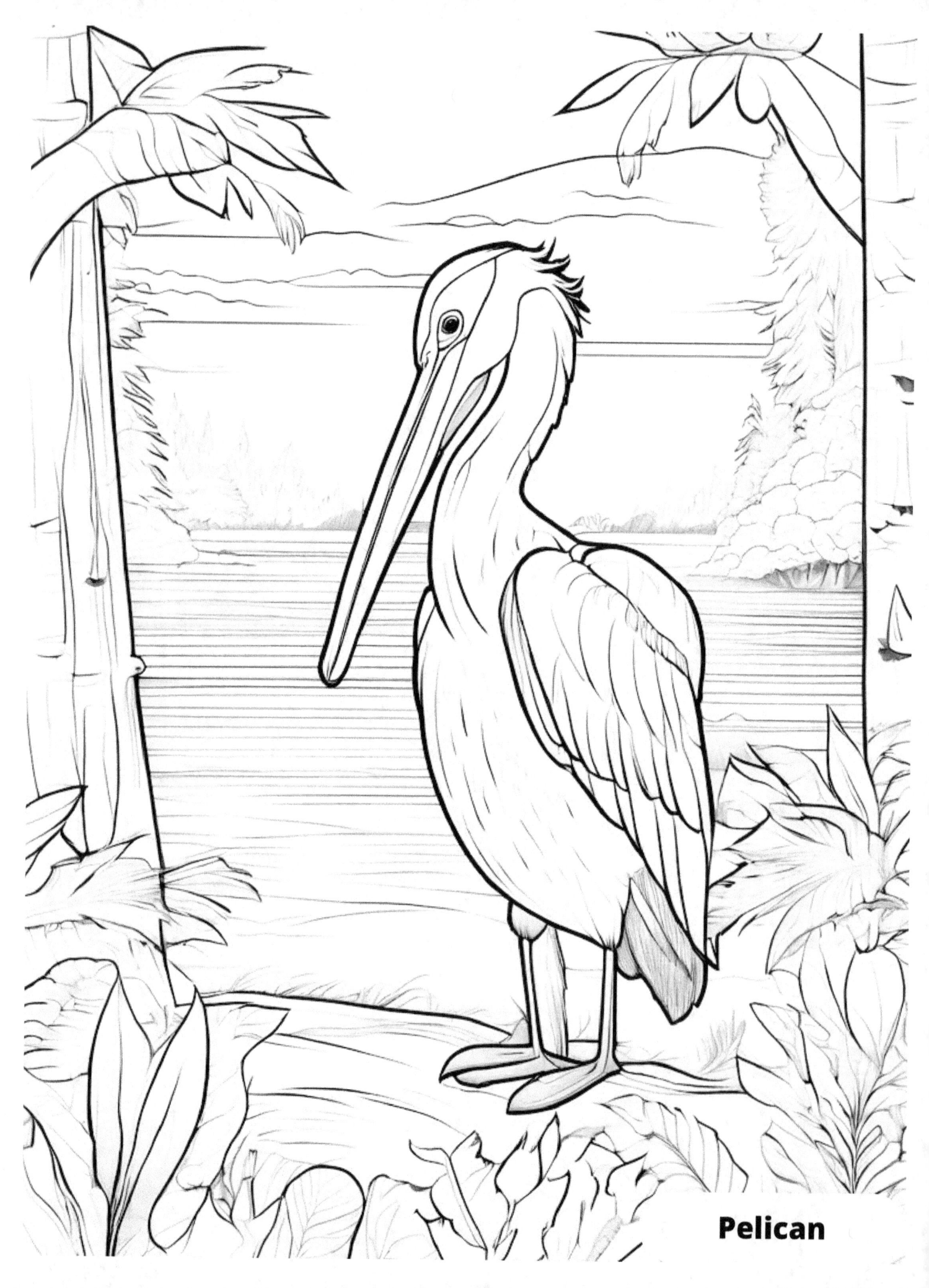

Pelican

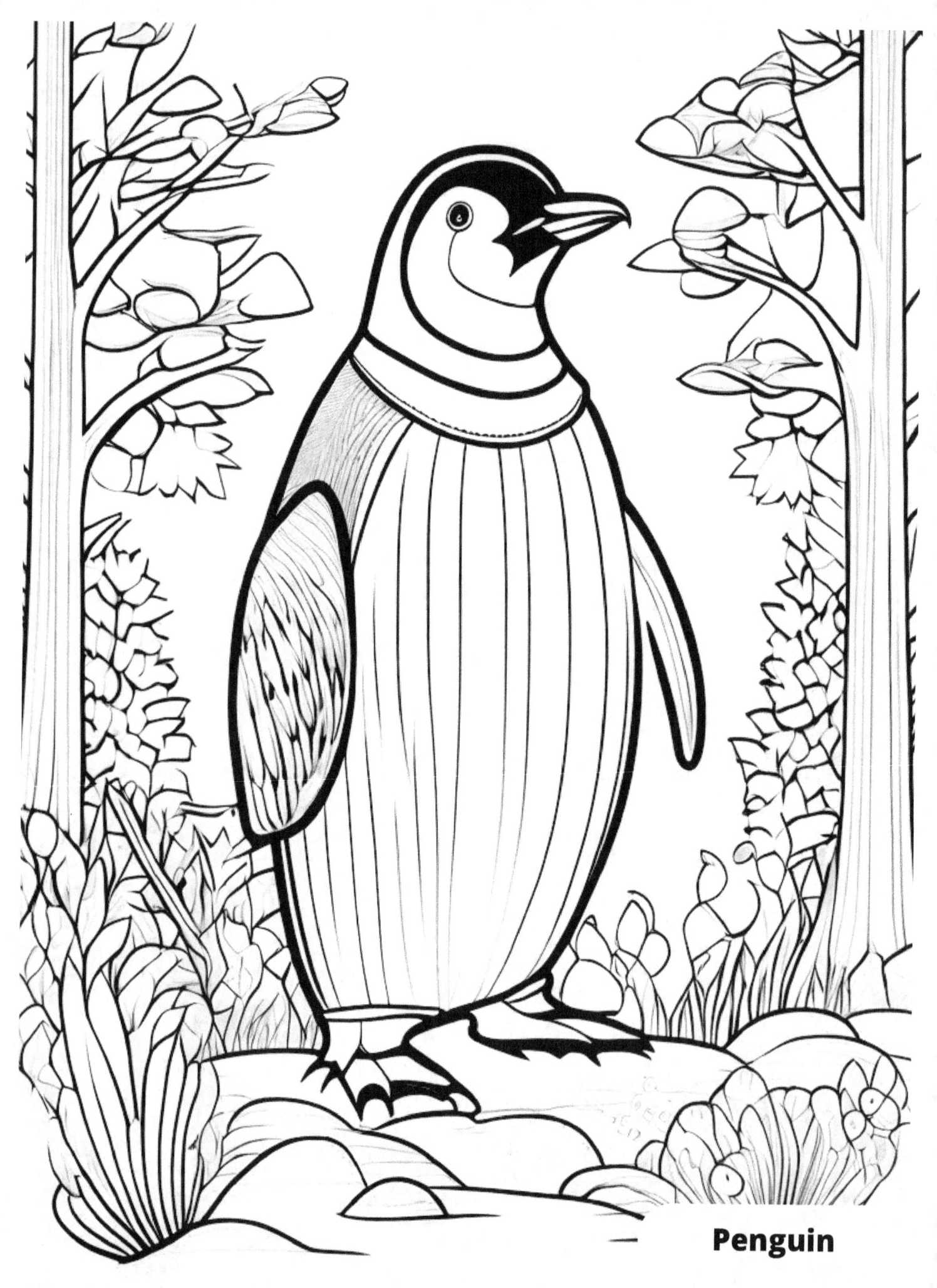

Penguin

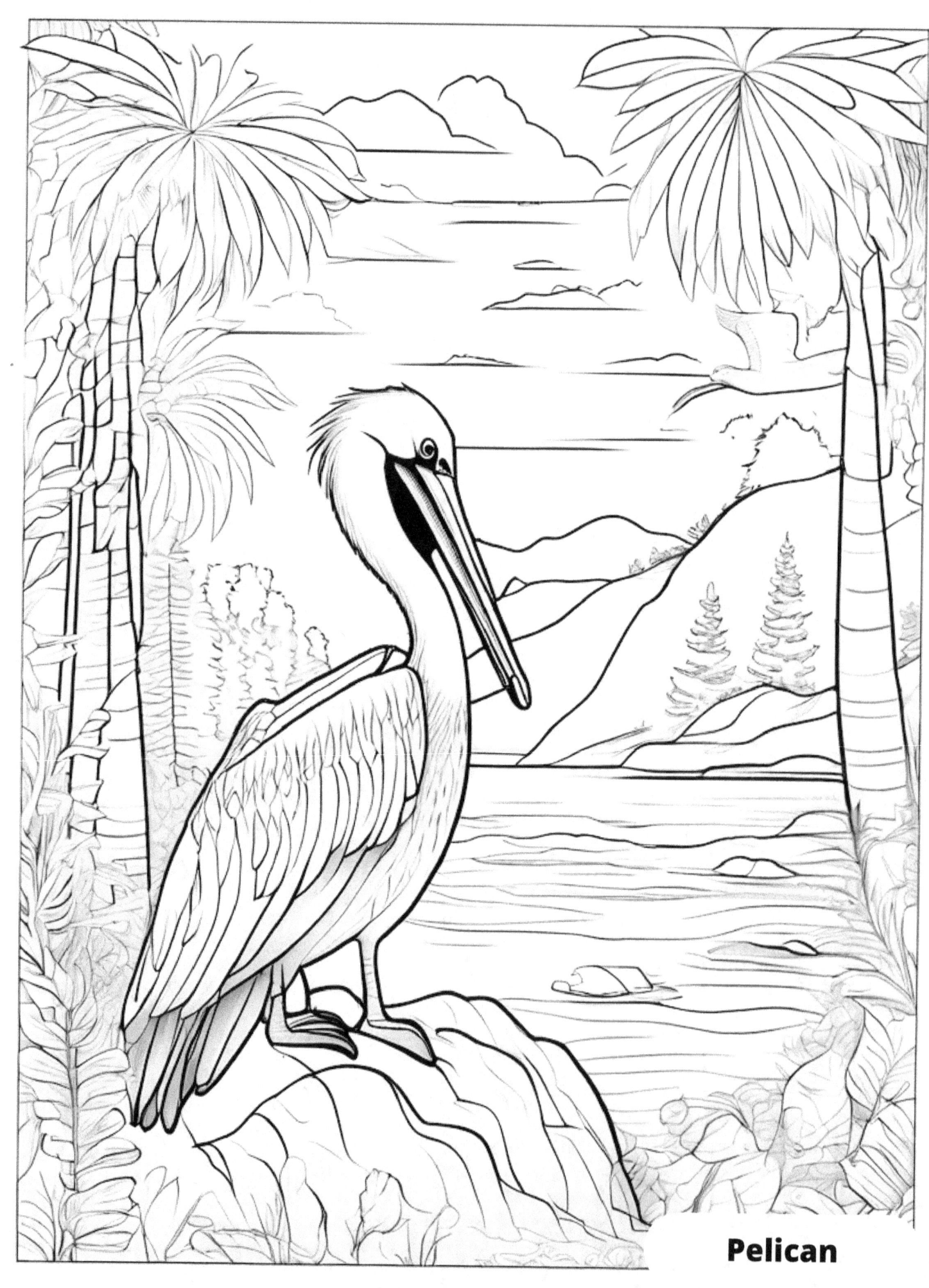

Pelican

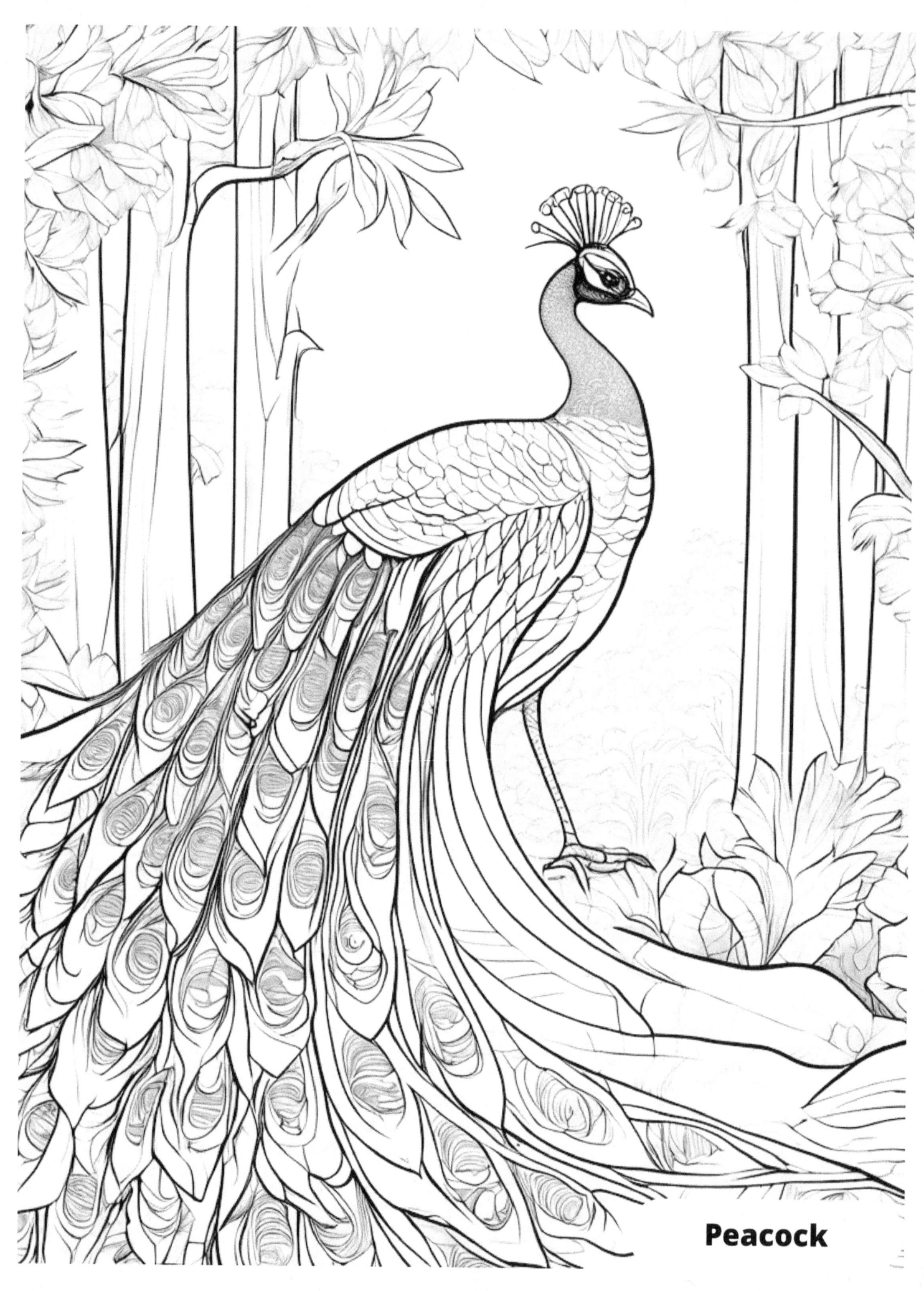

Peacock

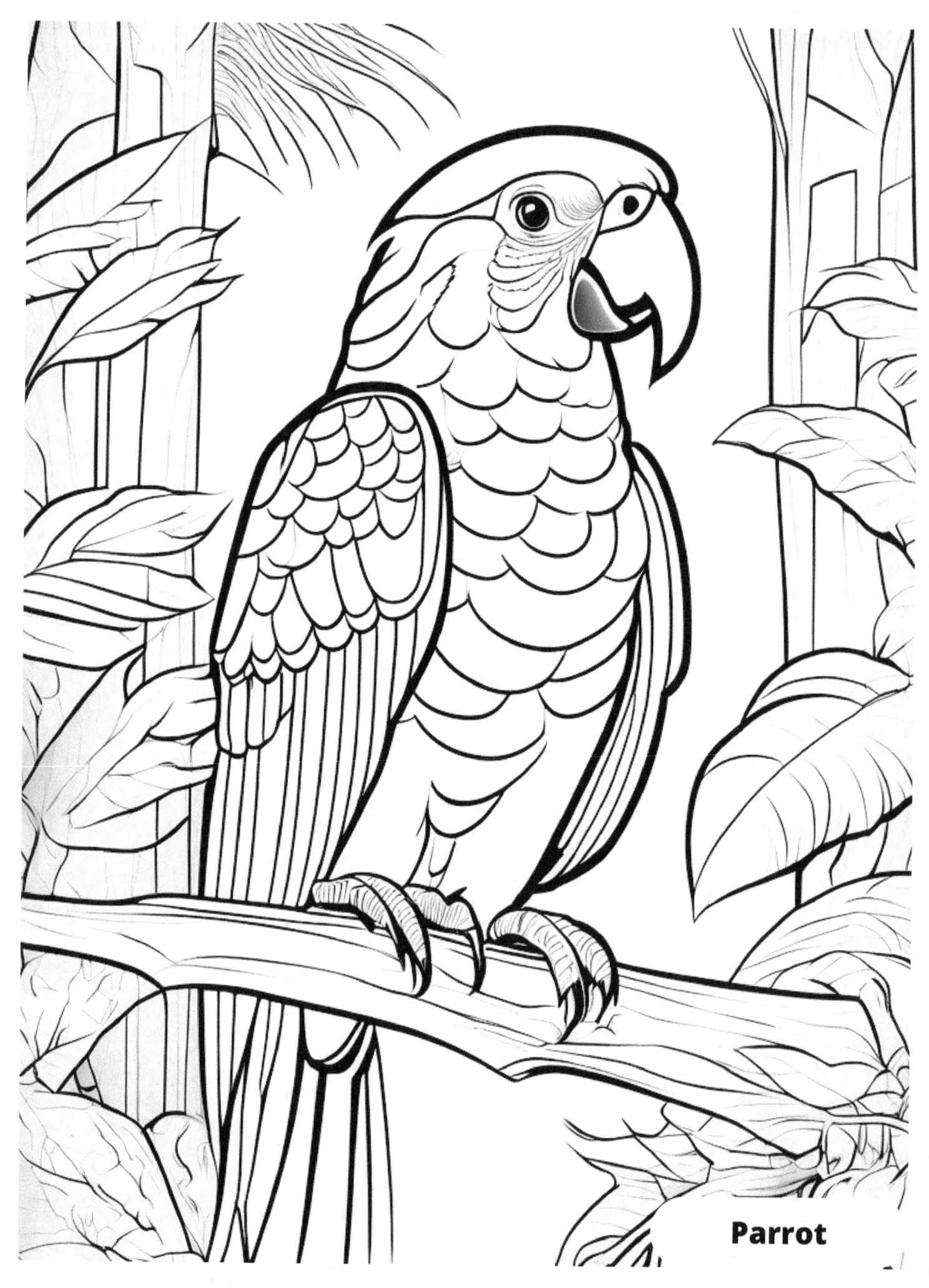

Parrot

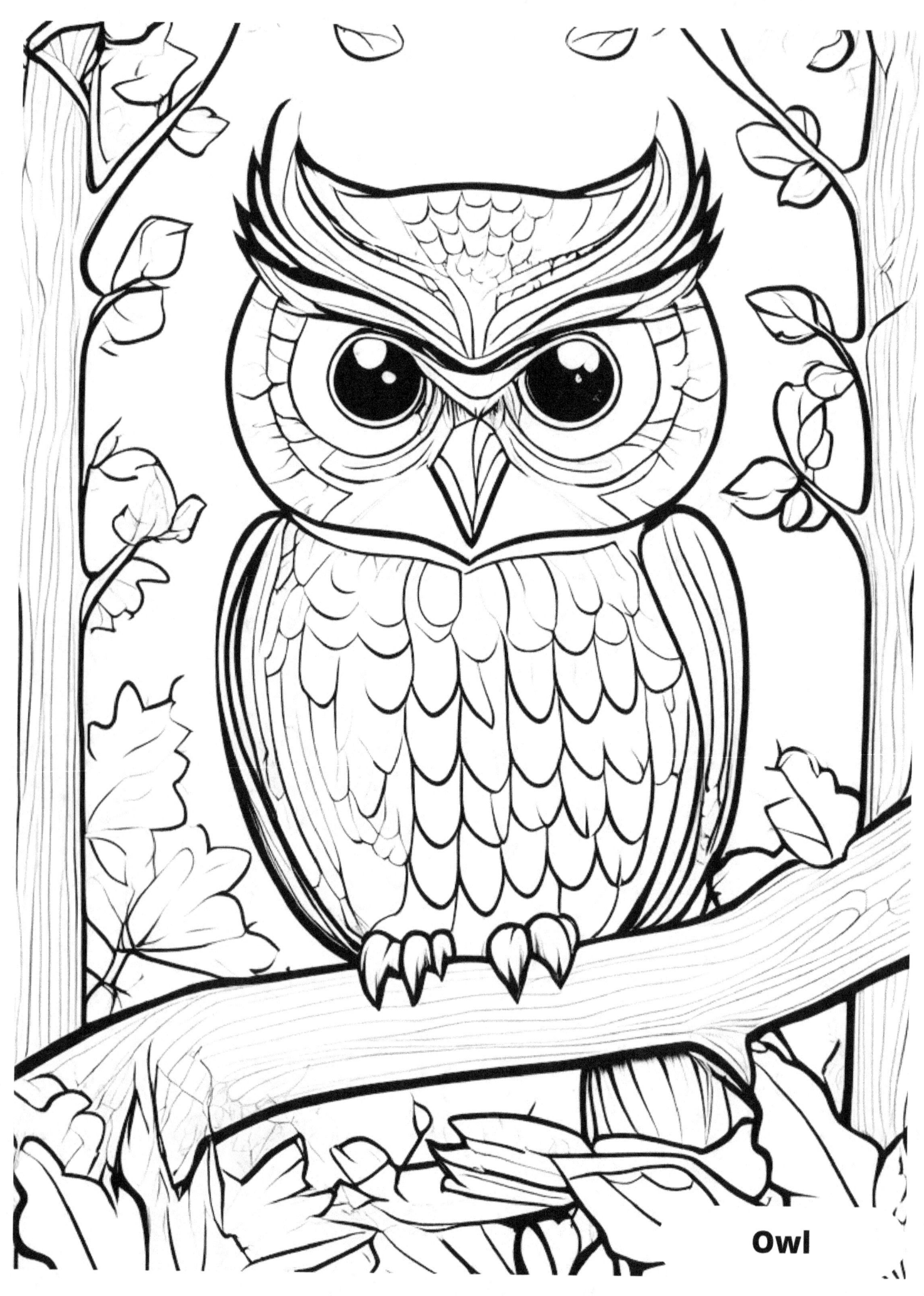

Owl

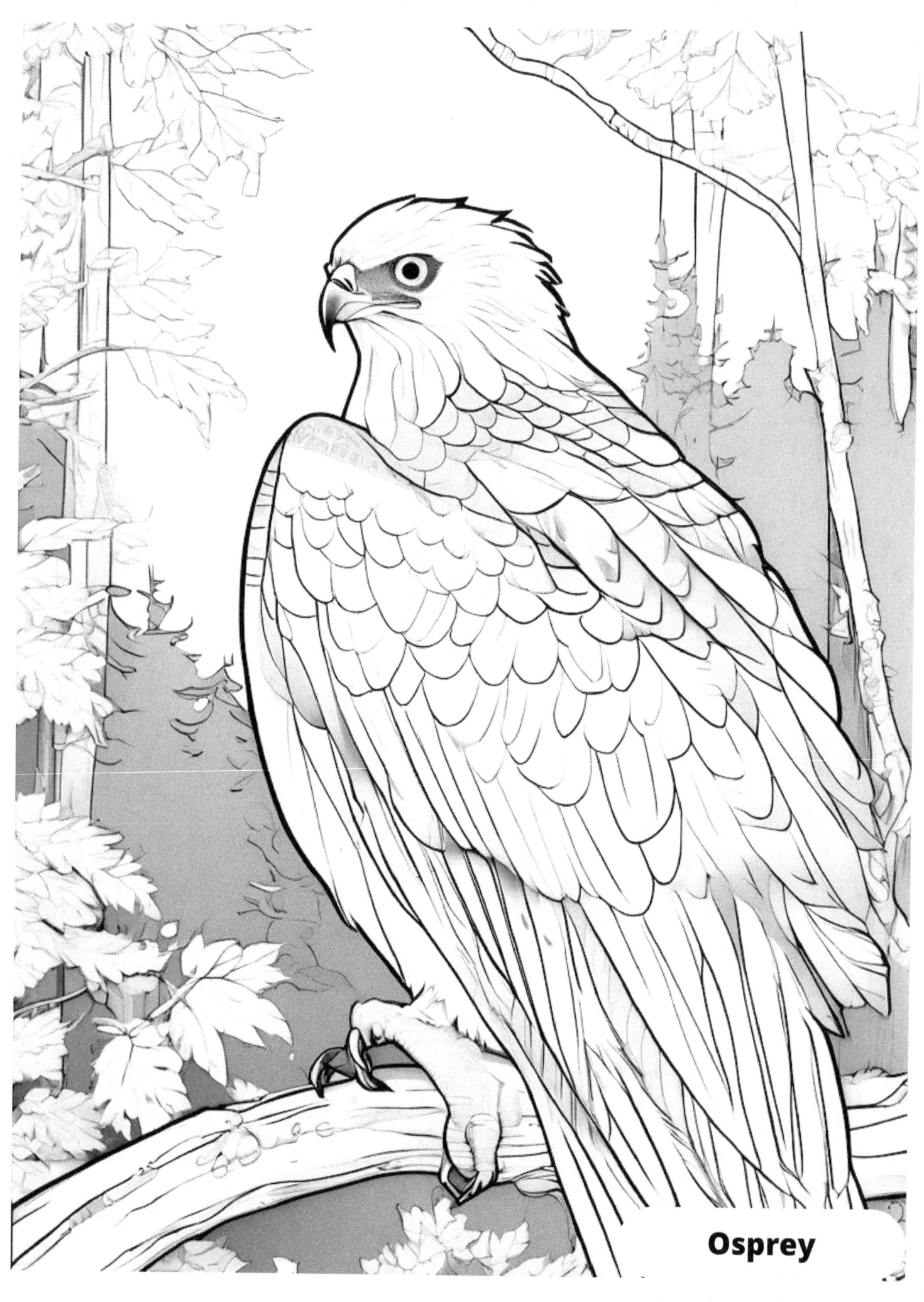

Osprey

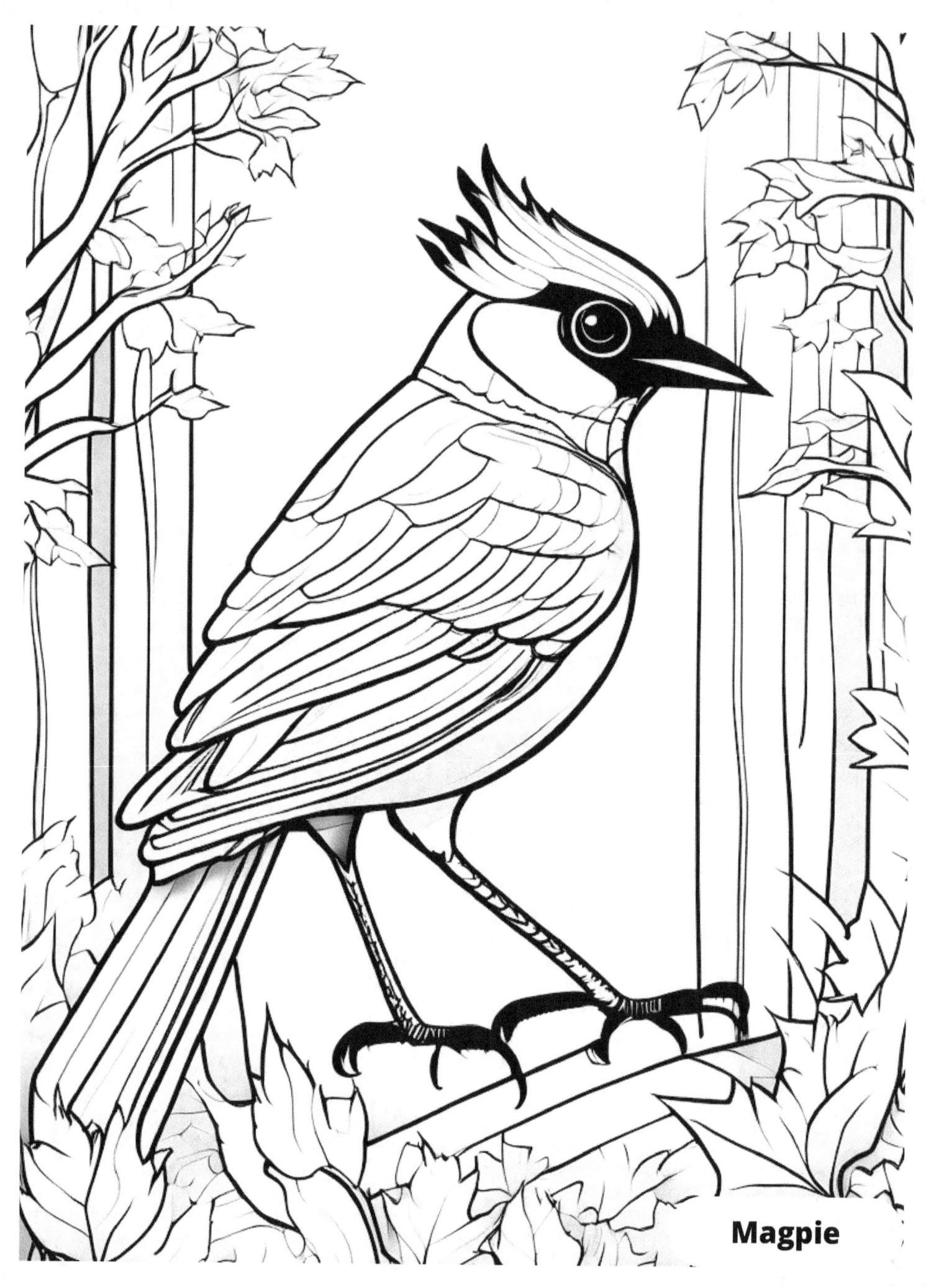

Magpie

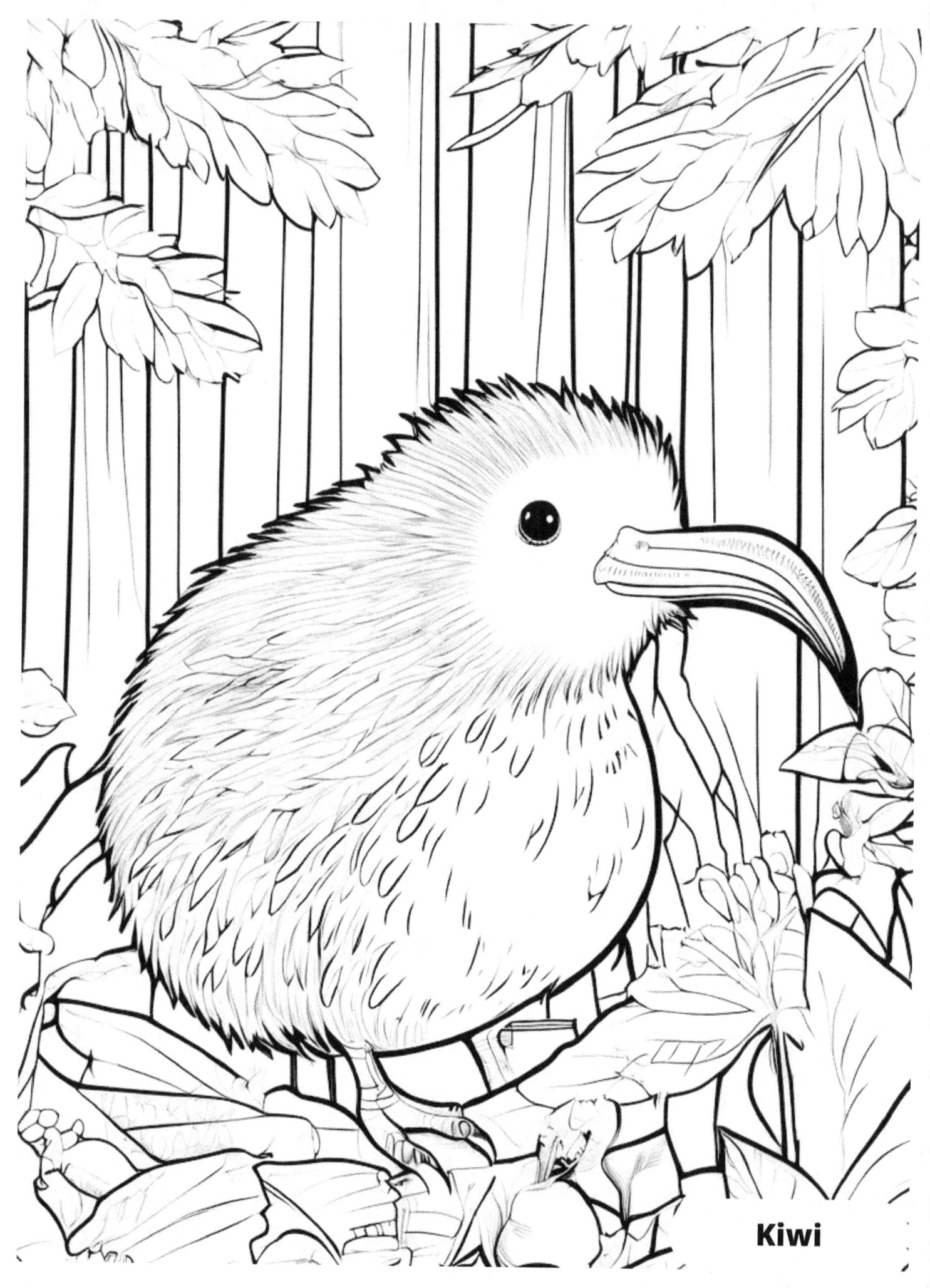

Kiwi

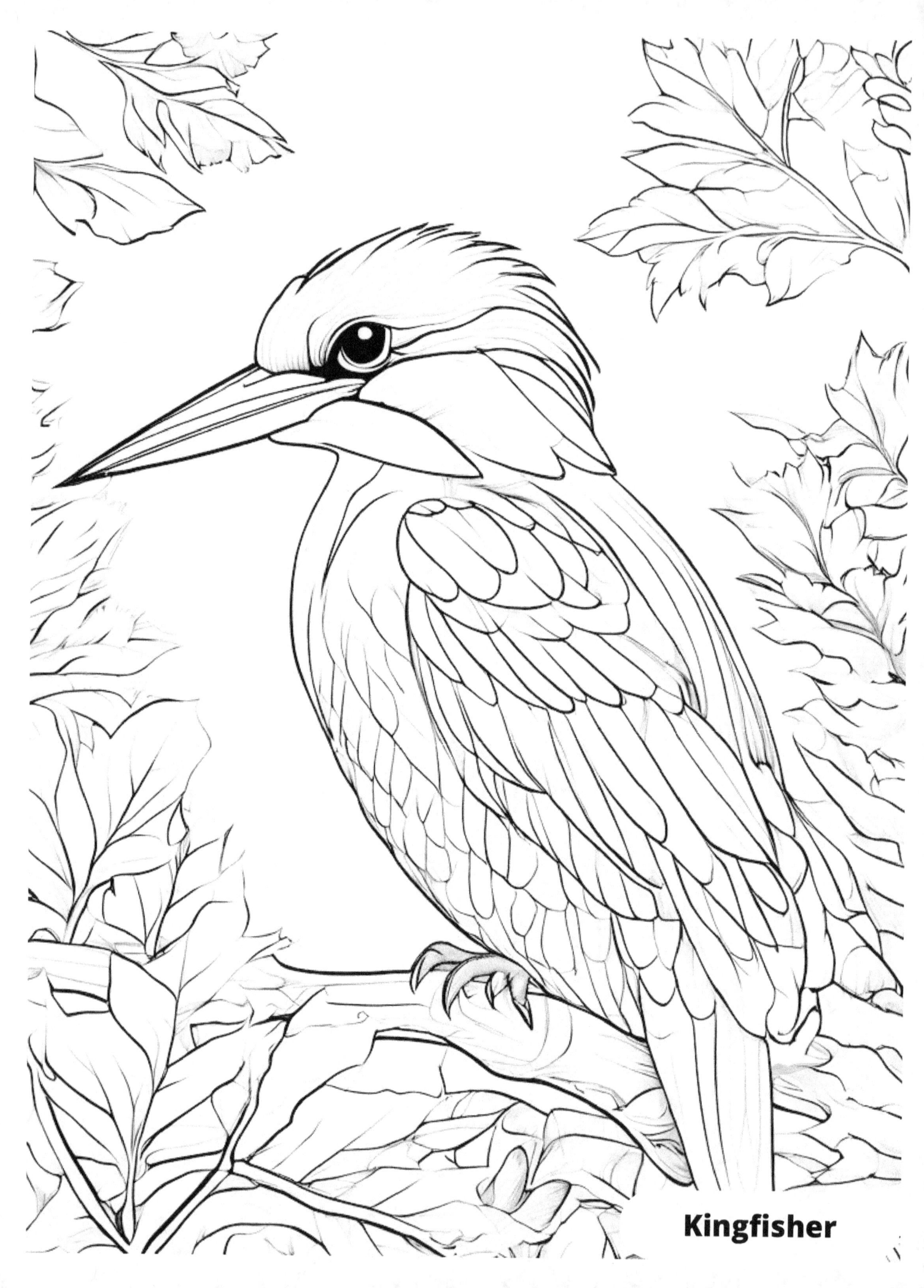

Kingfisher

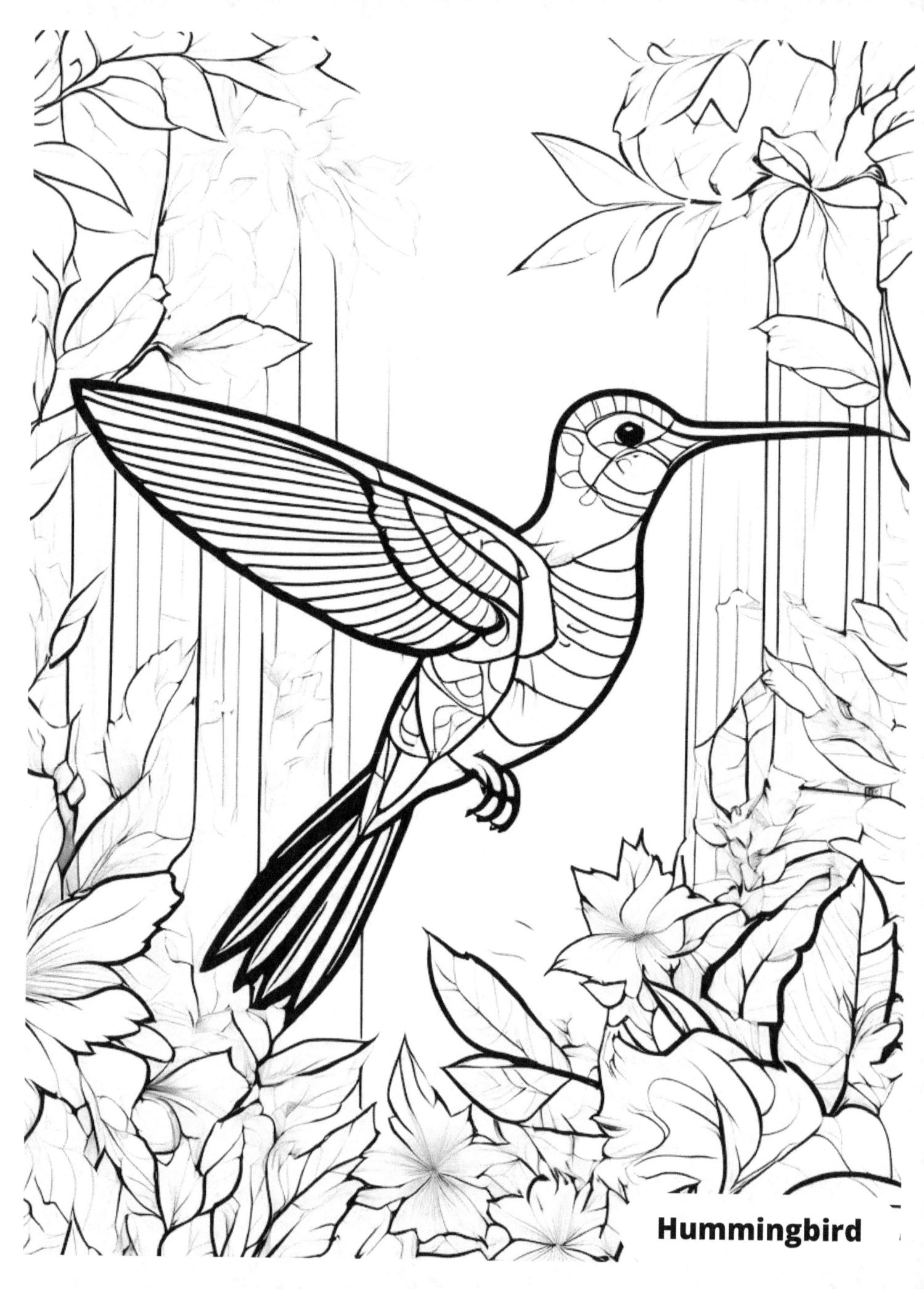

Hummingbird

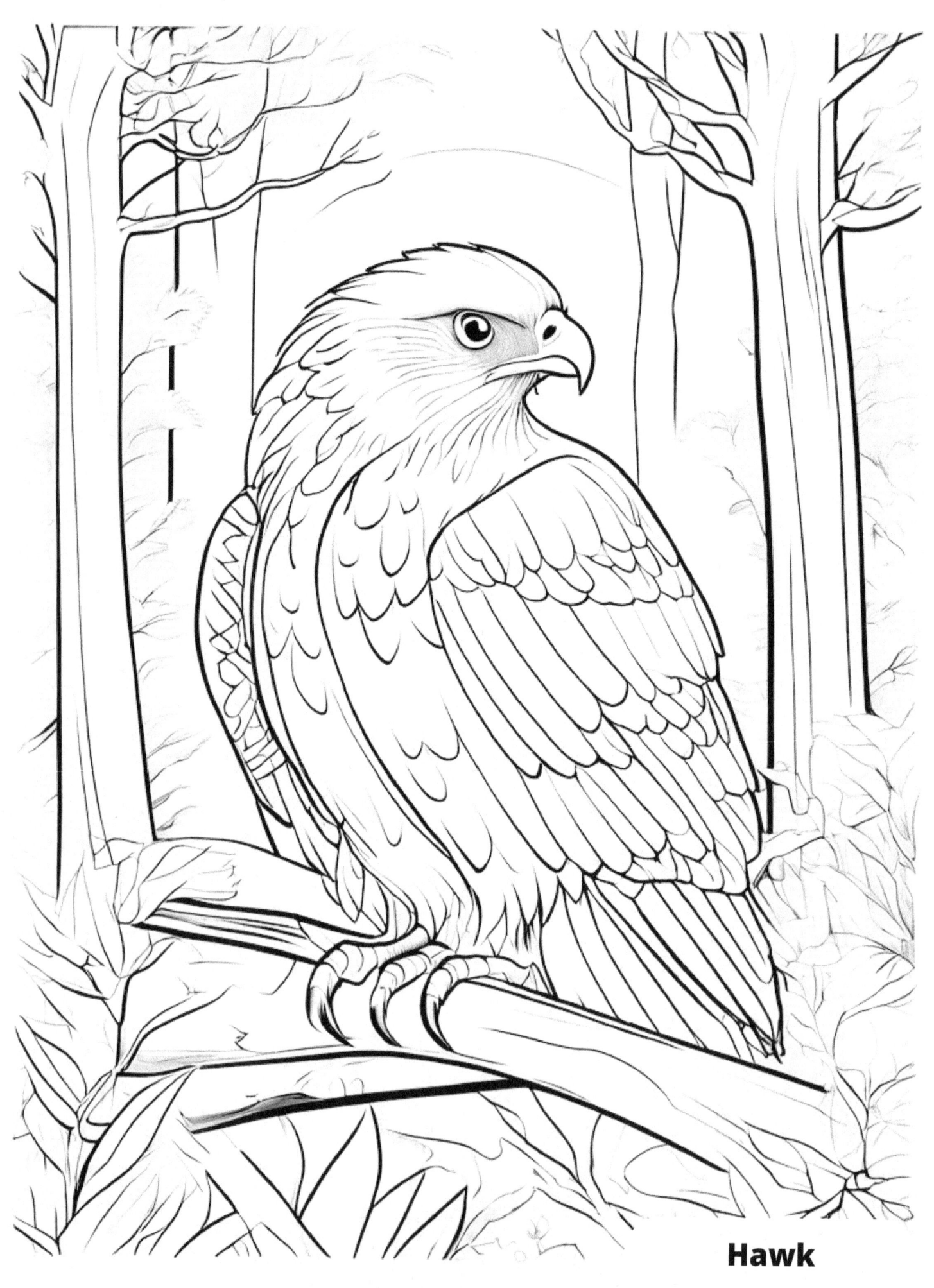

Hawk

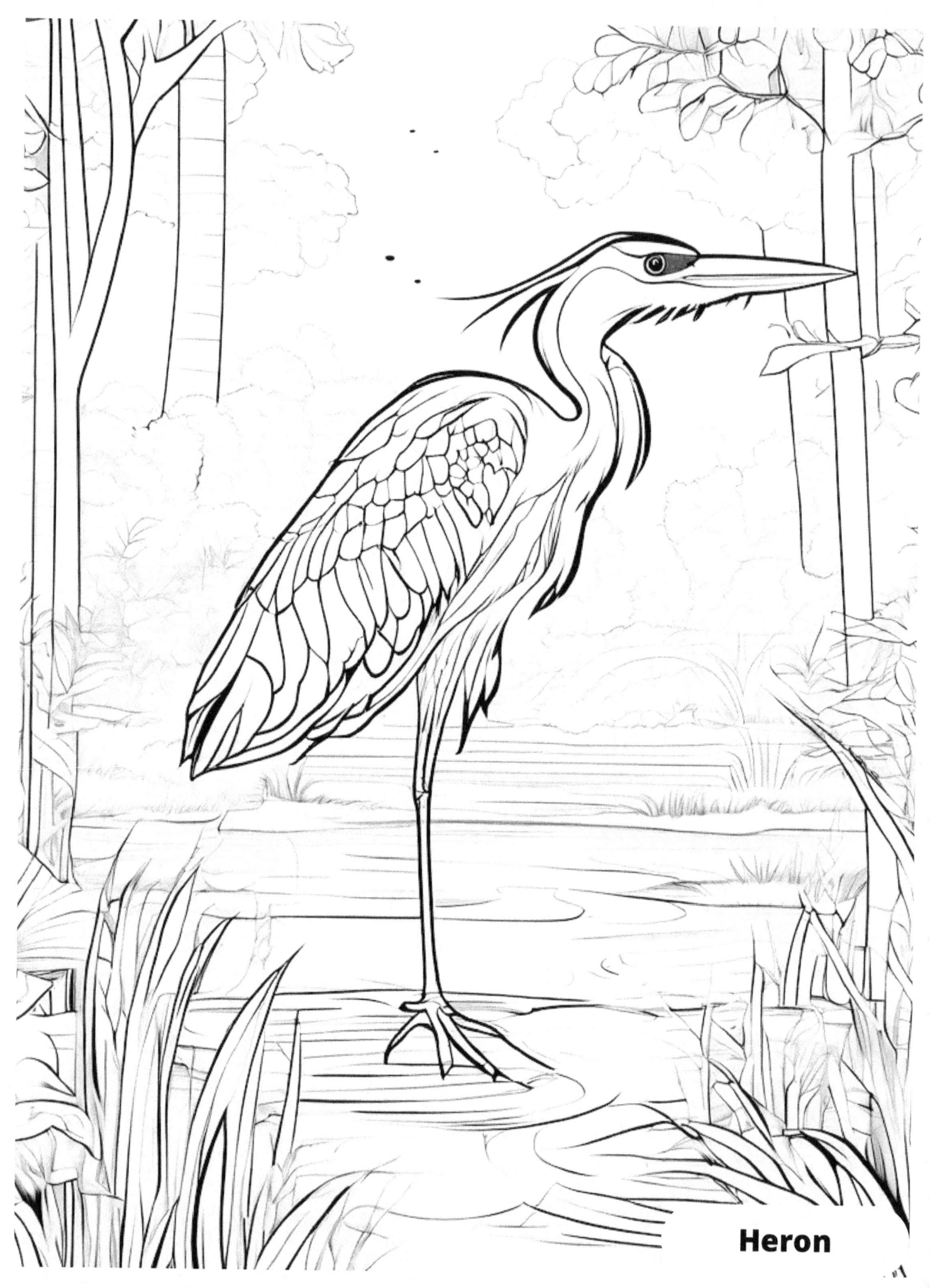

Heron

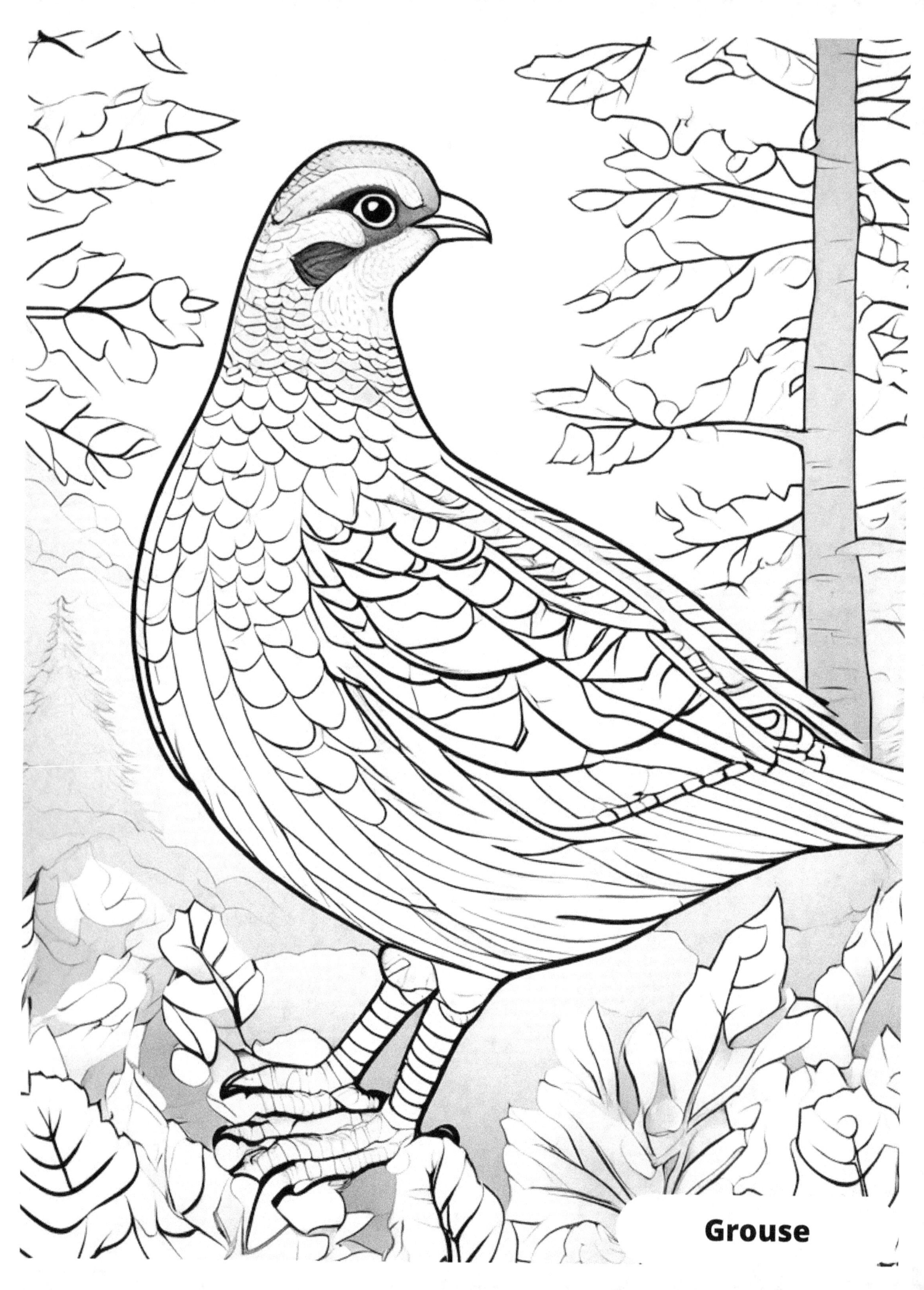

Grouse

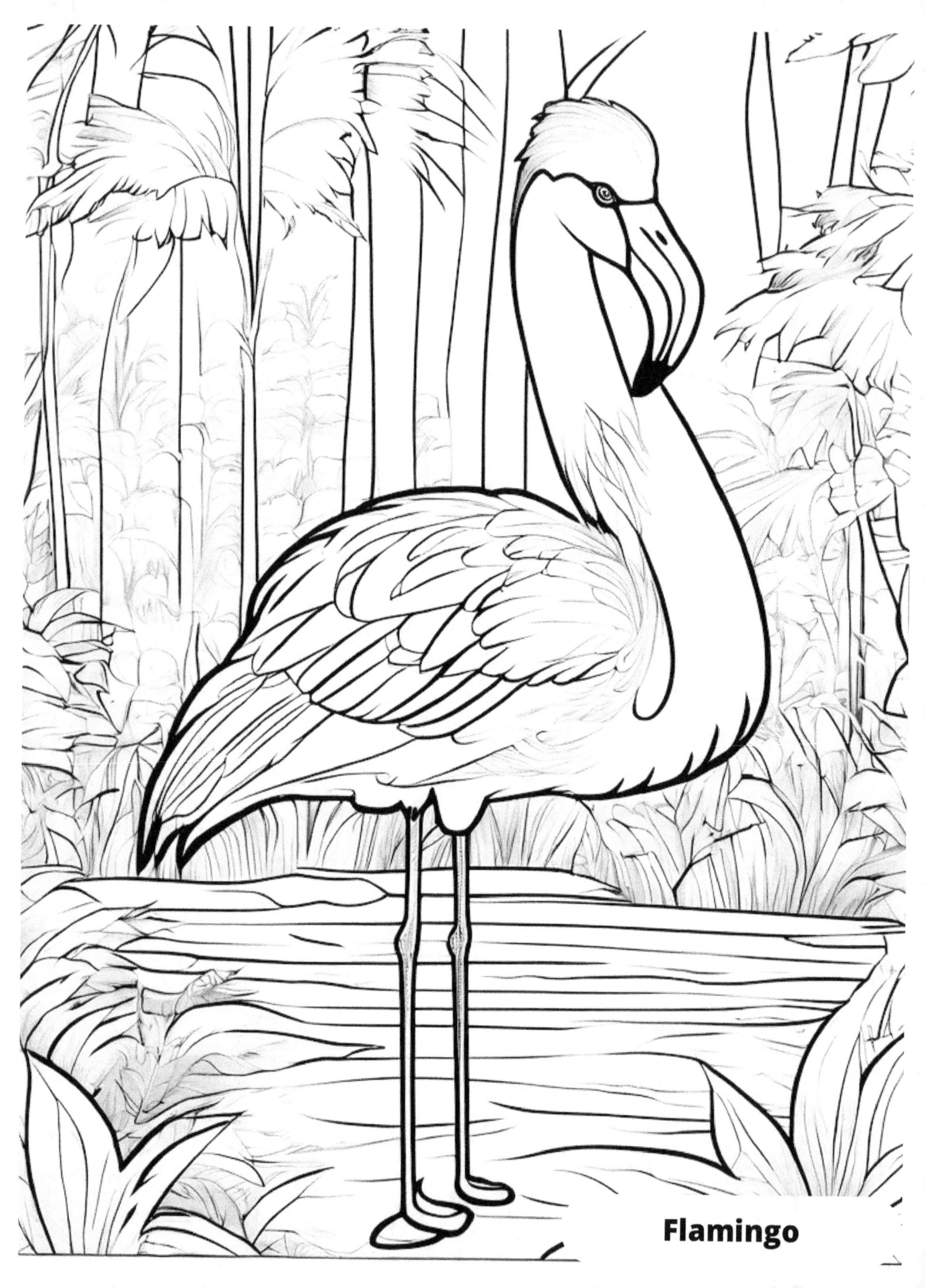

Flamingo

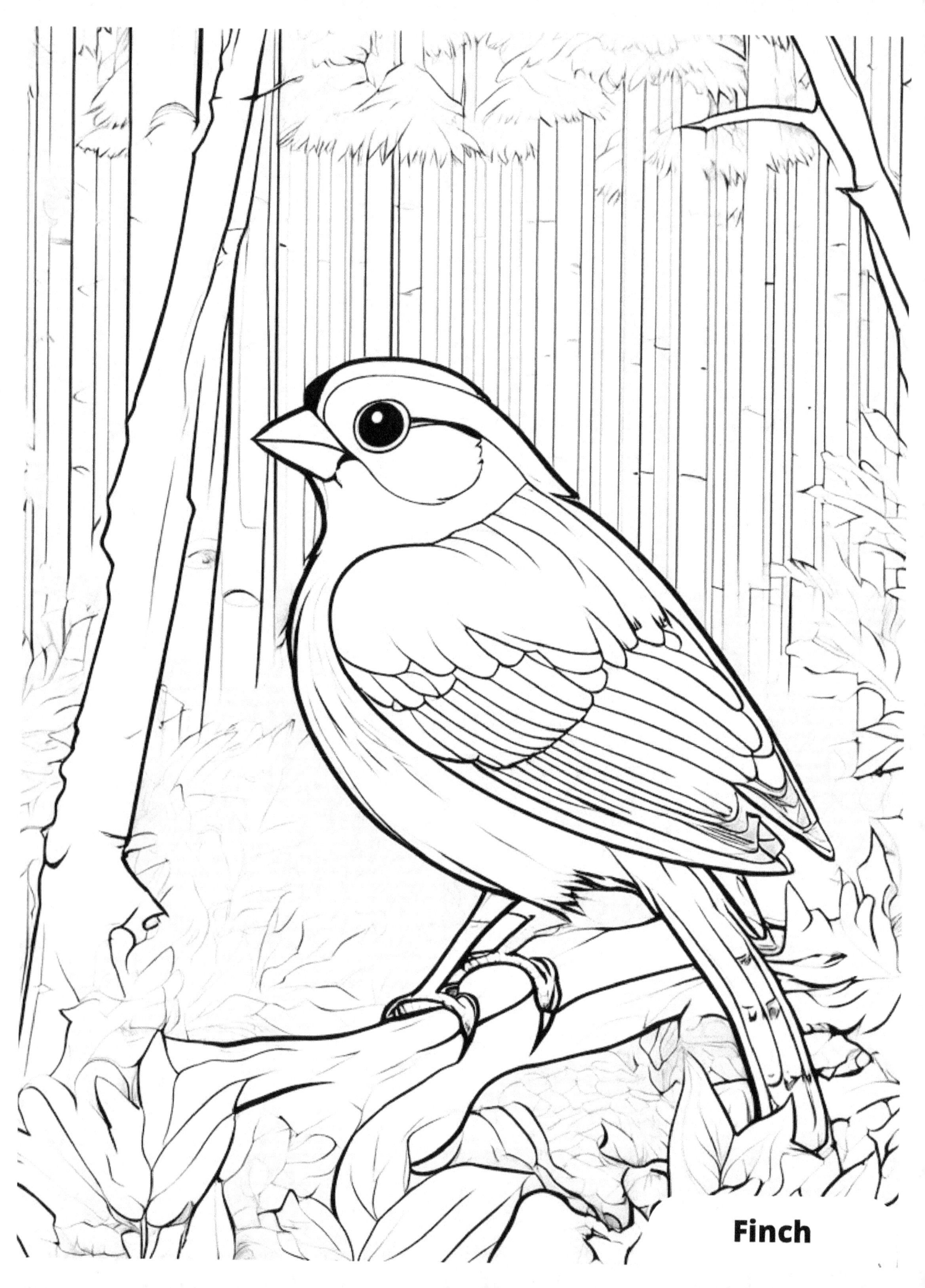

Finch

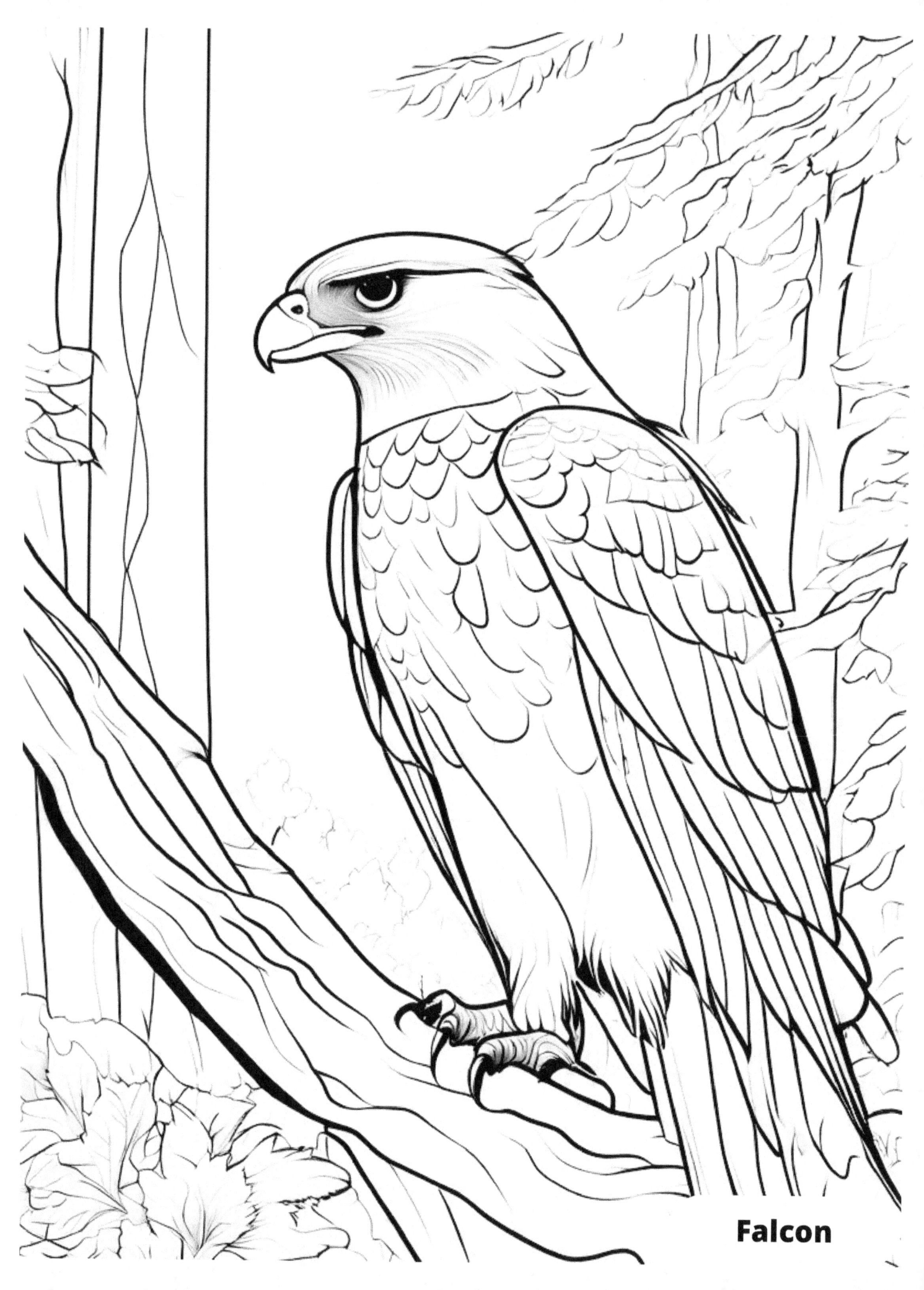

Falcon

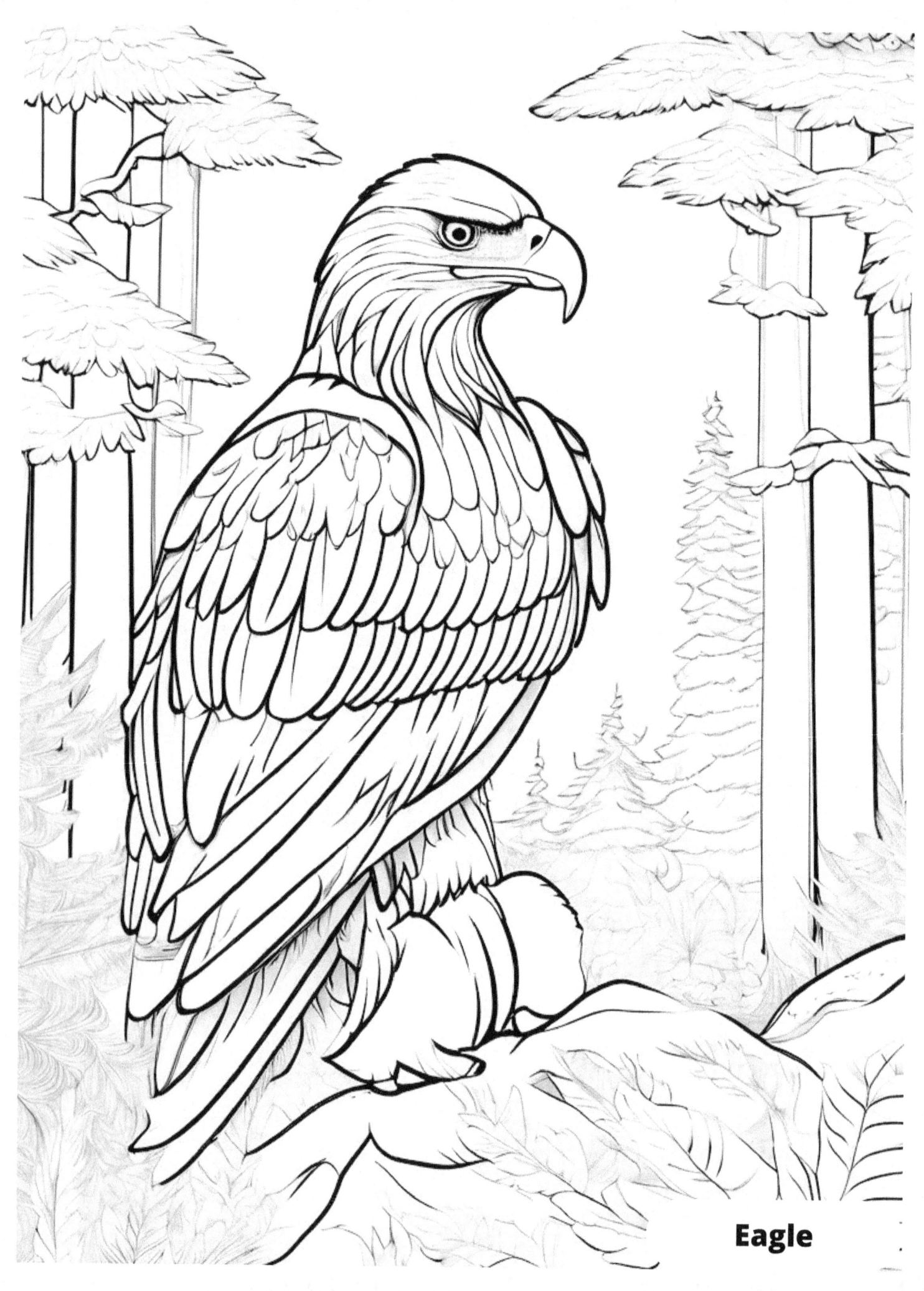

Eagle

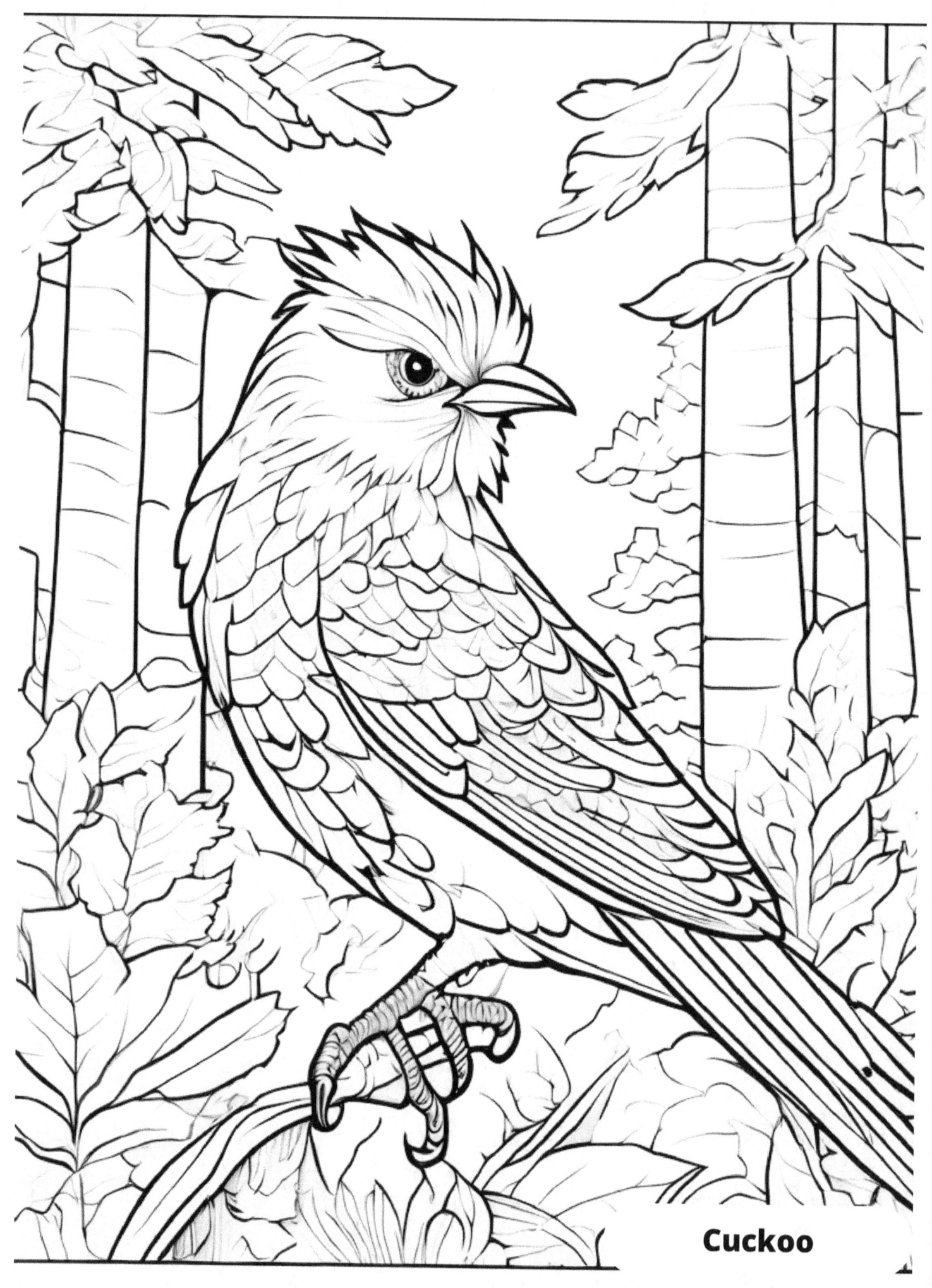

Cuckoo

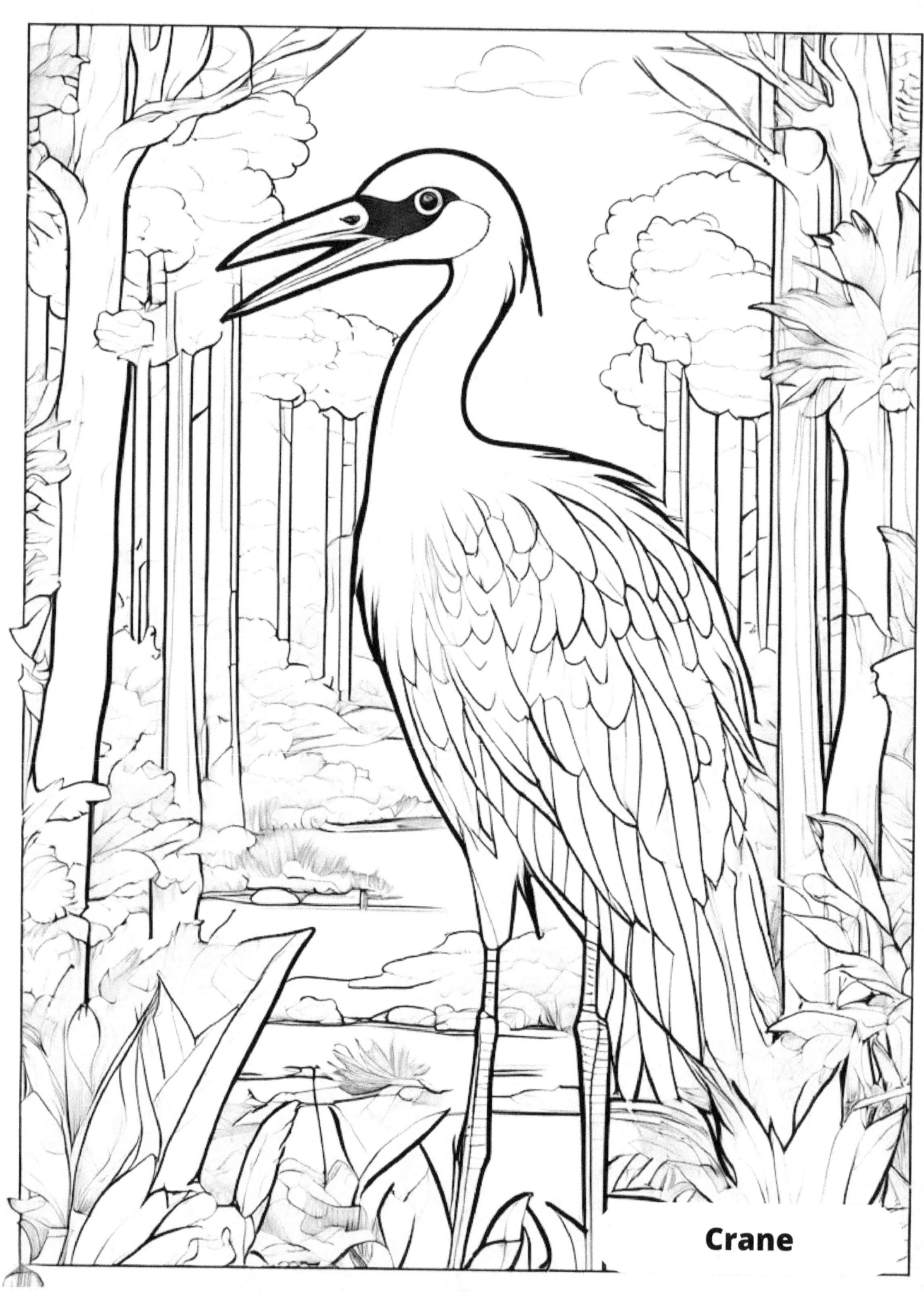

Crane

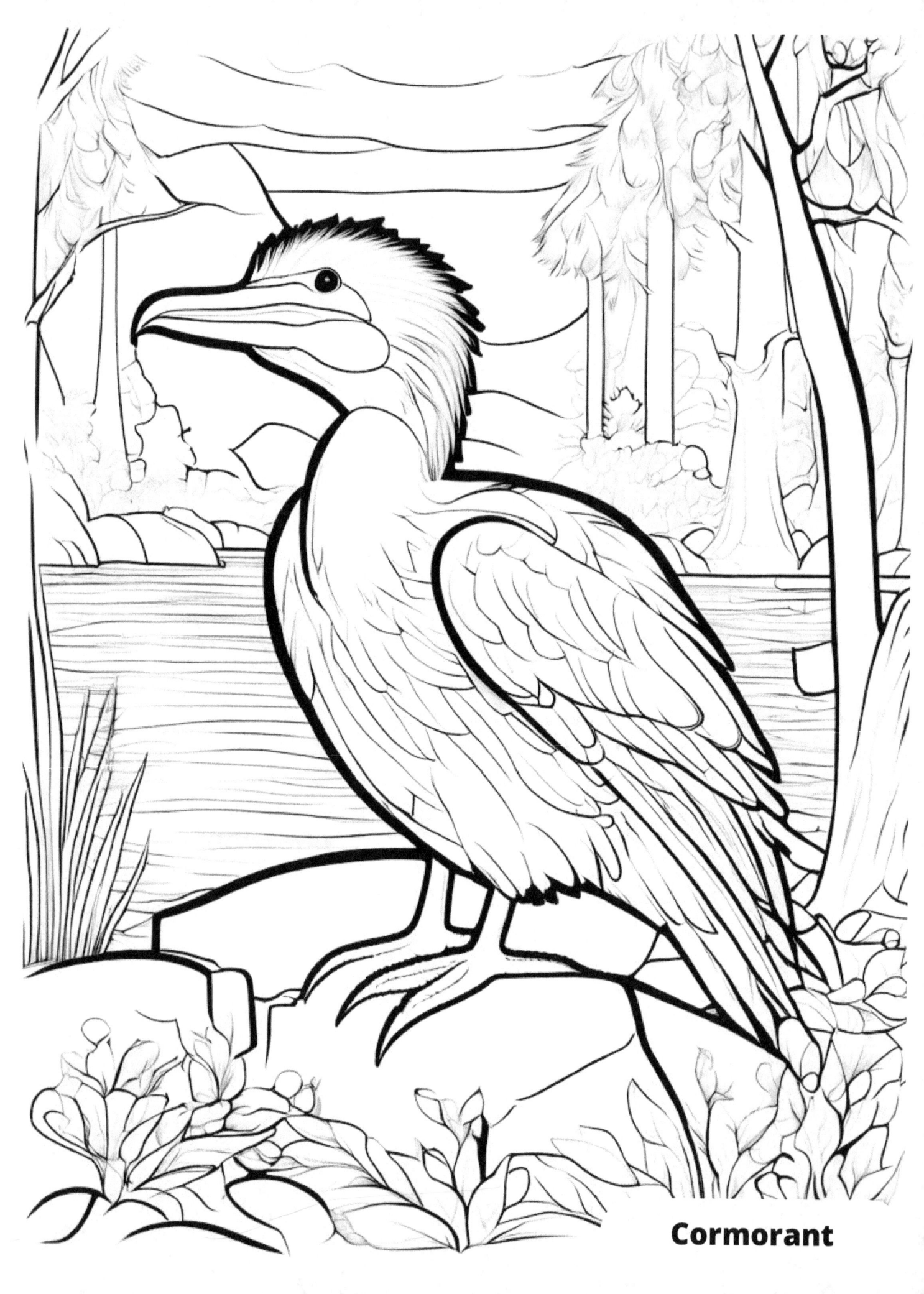

Cormorant

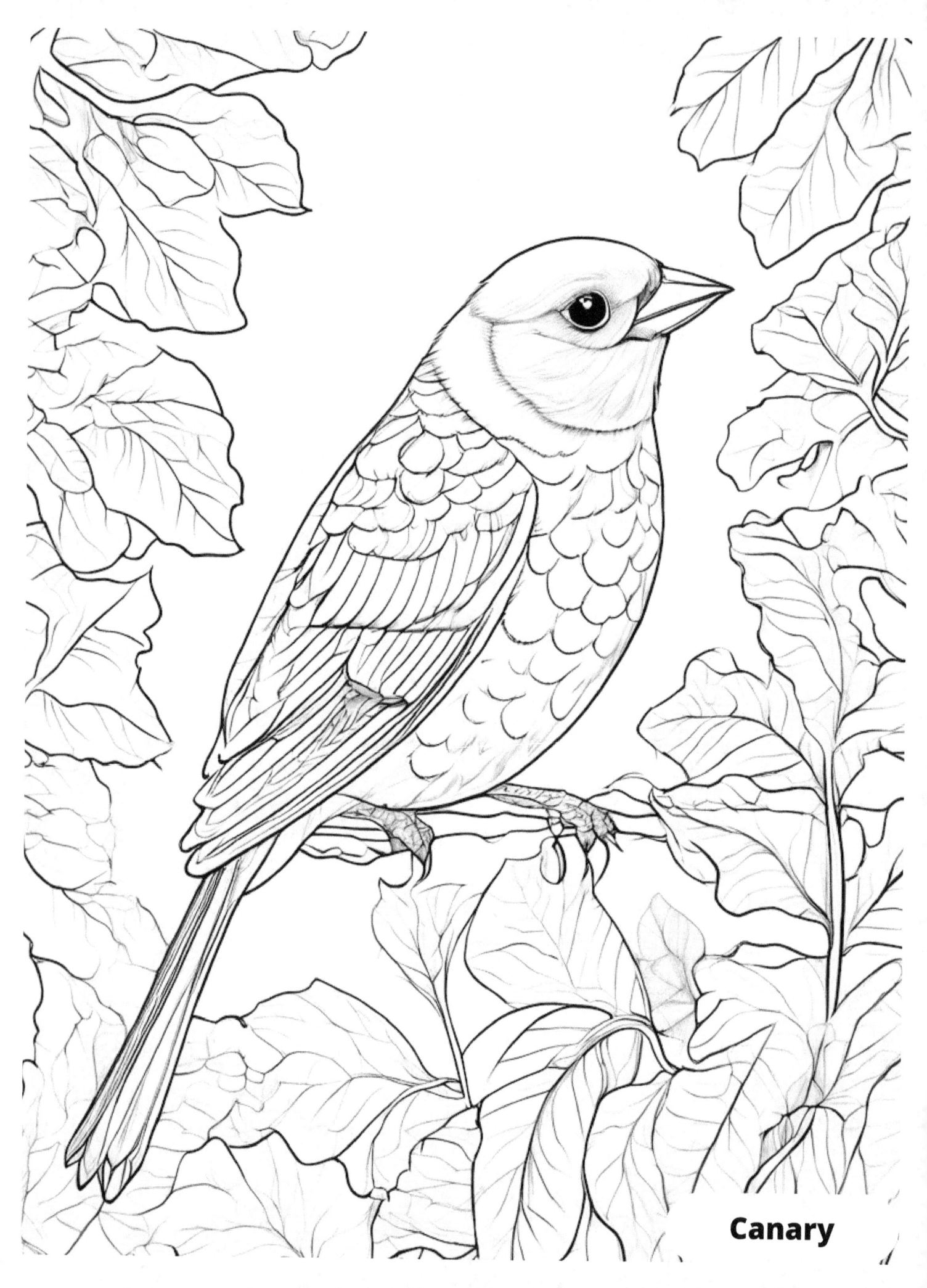

Canary

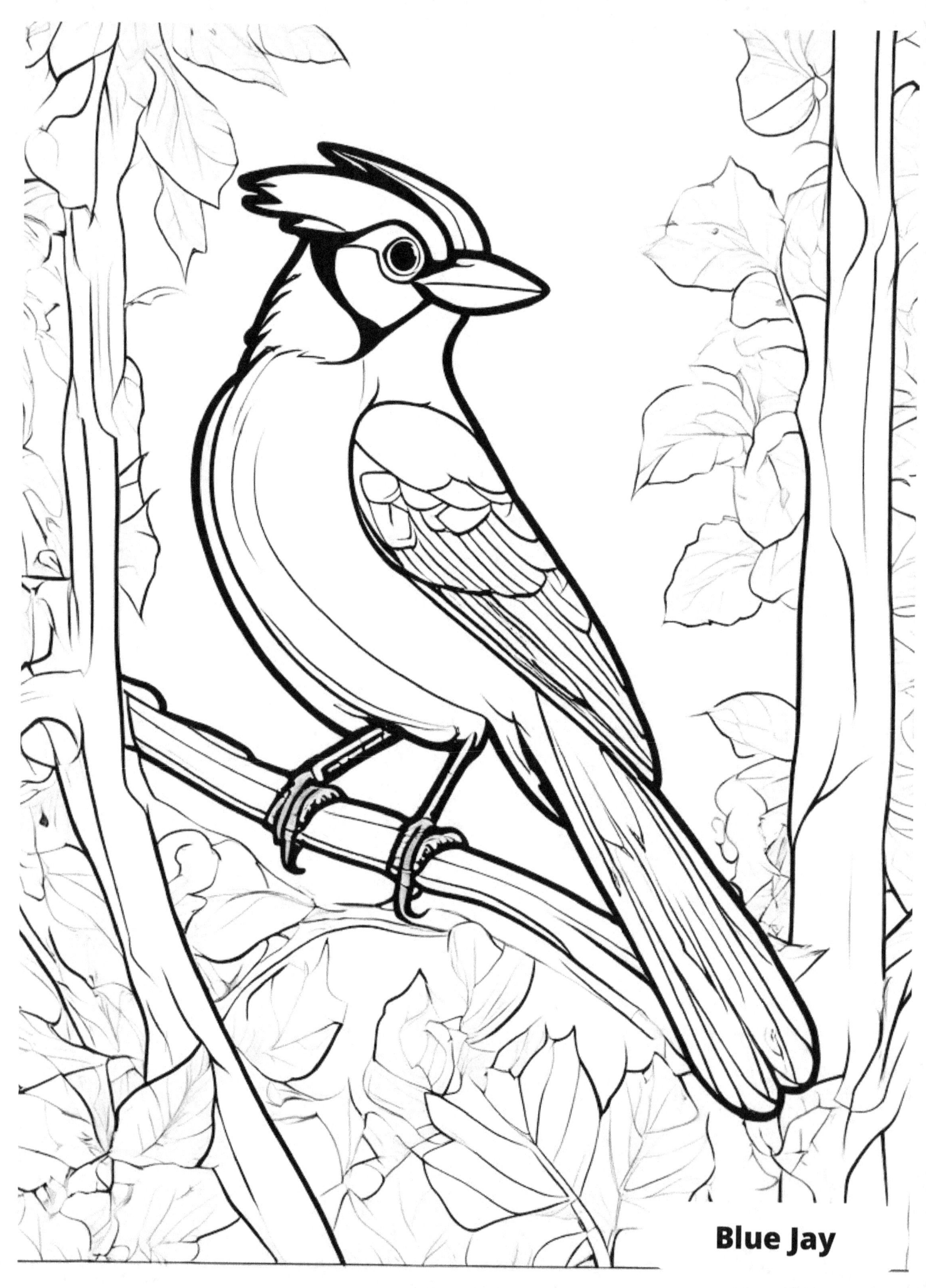

Blue Jay